Defense Purchases and

Regional Growth

Studies of Government Finance

TITLES PUBLISHED

Defense Purchases and

Regional Growth

ROGER E. BOLTON

Studies of Government Finance

THE BROOKINGS INSTITUTION

WASHINGTON, D.C.

THE BROOKINGS INSTITUTION is an independent organization devoted to nonpartisan research, education, and publication in economics, government, foreign policy, and the social sciences generally. Its principal purposes are to aid in the development of sound public policies and to promote public understanding of issues of national importance.

The Institution was founded December 8, 1927, to merge the activities of the Institute for Government Research, founded in 1916, the Institute of Economics, founded in 1922, and the Robert Brookings Graduate School of Economics and Government, founded in 1924.

The general administration of the Institution is the responsibility of a self-perpetuating Board of Trustees. The trustees are likewise charged with maintaining the independence of the staff and fostering the most favorable conditions for creative research and education. The immediate direction of the policies, program, and staff of the Institution is vested in the President, assisted by the division directors and an advisory council, chosen from the professional staff of the Institution.

In publishing a study, the Institution presents it as a competent treatment of a subject worthy of public consideration. The interpretations and conclusions in such publications are those of the author or authors and do not purport to represent the views of the other staff members, officers, or trustees of the Brookings Institution.

Foreword

THE EFFECT OF DEFENSE EXPENDITURES on regional growth in the United States has been the subject of considerable discussion in recent years, but very little has been done to provide quantitative measurements of the impact. In this volume, Roger E. Bolton presents a simple model of regional growth and provides estimates of the contribution of defense income to this growth in the period from 1952 to 1962. These estimates show the differential impact of the nation's defense program by states and by region.

This study was originally made as a doctoral dissertation at Harvard University under the Economics of Public Expenditures Project, sponsored by the National Committee on Government Finance of the Brookings Institution. During part of the time the study was written, the author was a Danforth Fellow at Harvard University.

The author's greatest professional debt in the preparation of this study is to Otto Eckstein of Harvard, who supervised the study in its earlier stages as a doctoral dissertation, and supplied advice, criticism, and encouragement from the beginning to the end.

The author was an employee of the Office of the Secretary of Defense during the summer of 1962 and received helpful suggestions for this study from Henry Glass, the Economic Advisor to the Comptroller, Richard Walsh and Phil O'Deen of the Economic Advisor's Office, Sam Clark, and Carrel Todd. However, the views presented are not necessarily those of the Department of Defense, or any of its personnel.

The author also wishes to express his appreciation for the assistance he received from James S. Duesenberry, Edward F. Denison, Clopper Almon, Frederick Bell, and Charles Trozzo. James Prescott was of invaluable help in programming the computer calculations, and the Harvard Department of Economics provided some of the computer time required under National Science Foundation Grant GP-2723. The reading committee—consisting of Richard Goode, Robert Graham, and Murray Weidenbaum—made numerous helpful comments. The manuscript was edited by Verrick O. French. The author wishes to express his greatest debt to his wife, Julia, for her patient and enthusiastic encouragement to complete this study.

This study is part of a special program of research and education on taxation and public expenditures, supervised by the National Committee on Government Finance and financed by a special grant from the Ford Foundation.

The views expressed in this study are the author's and are not presented as the views of the National Committee on Government Finance or its Advisory Committee, or the staff members, officers, or trustees of the Brookings Institution, or the Ford Foundation.

Robert D. Calkins
President

December 1965
Washington, D.C.

Studies of Government Finance

Studies of Government Finance is a special program of research and education in taxation and government expenditures at the federal, state, and local levels. These studies are under the supervision of the National Committee on Government Finance appointed by the trustees of the Brookings Institution, and are supported by a special grant from the Ford Foundation.

Contents

Text Tables

Maps

Figure

General Appendix Tables

CHAPTER I

Introduction and Summary

THE PAST SEVERAL YEARS have seen much discussion of the regional distribution of defense expenditures in the United States. There are two general reasons for this. The possibility of disarmament has led many to ponder the heavy dependence of certain areas on defense demand, and the current pattern of defense expenditures differs markedly from that of either World War II or the Korean War. The most dramatic change has been an extreme shift in military prime contracts, but the regional distribution of military and civilian employee payrolls has shifted as well. Changes during the 1950's had important repercussions for regional growth simply because they were large enough to amount to significant shifts in demand, and because defense activity is an important source of income for certain areas.

In adjusting to new requirements of warfare—particularly to changes in the nature of weapons and in geographical requirements for installation sites—the armed services drastically changed the geographical impact of defense purchases. Even with a rising defense budget in the later 1950's, these changes caused an absolute decline in defense demand in some areas and a relative decline in many others. Such changes were bound to elicit protests from areas whose "defense business" fell off. Moreover, defense procurement —the largest and most widely discussed part of purchases—has traditionally been complex and uncertain enough to require *negotiation* of most contracts, rather than formal advertising and low-bid selection. Negotiation allows more discretion in awards, and regardless of whether geographical preferences influence the awarding of contracts, discretion opens the way for criticism by unsuccessful bidders. Those who saw their defense business going elsewhere in the 1950's blamed their losses on an excessive concern with "efficiency," and on "politics"—which they felt was especially encouraged by discretionary awards. Some argued that the available discretion should be used to *prevent,* not encourage, radical changes in regional distribution. It ought to be pointed out, however, that the use of formal advertising rather than negotiation actually increased slightly in the period after Korea. But in the need to develop entirely new weapons and technical processes, the factors shaping the distribution of contracts became much more subtle than the mere existence of capacity, since new capacity had to be created. As it happened, New England, the West, and the South were able to develop this capacity at the expense of some older areas with more traditional manufacturing industries.

Certain areas, which have been termed "defense babies," grew very rapidly in the post-Korean period. In these places a few initial contracts seemed to generate a remarkably rapid expansion in industrial capacity. Some people were bound to ask, "Why can't it happen to us?" and representatives of hard-pressed "depressed areas," though surely less sanguine about great booms, said, "Why not throw a little our way, at least until we get back on our feet?"

Purpose and General Outline of the Study

The regional impact of defense expenditures has understandably commanded wide attention as an economic issue in recent years. But discussion of the public policy decisions involved has had to proceed mostly on intuitive grounds because it has been difficult to quantify either the amount of defense demand in different regions of the country or the extent of its contribution to economic growth. This study attempts to supply information of a quantitative nature—to develop evidence on which the public policy issues ought to be decided. But the complexity of the problem and the incompleteness of available data still limit such evidence to what must be viewed as estimates of uncertain reliability. Nevertheless, this study proceeds farther than have previous ones, and even allowing for a good deal of error in the estimates, it presents unmistakable evidence of differing impacts of defense purchases on regional growth in the United States.

More concretely, the study first outlines a simple theory of regional growth, specifies the variables which are crucial for the theory, and estimates the values of these variables using the available regional income data. This procedure is carried out for each state and census region, and for each of three alternative definitions of one of the theory's crucial variables. The theory, in its various forms, is then tested for its capacity to explain the economic growth of each state and region in the postwar period. All three variants were found to work about equally well. Chapters III and IV make up this part of the study.

The second major part of the study describes the procedure by which defense purchases were estimated for each state and region for the years from 1951 to 1962, and it includes a tabulation of these estimates. Because the figures derived in this long and detailed section must be considered uncertain estimates, much space is devoted to discussion of available data, and to consideration of the assumptions necessary to derive any reasonable figures at all. Here also, three alternative estimates are made for each state and year, in order to reveal the sensitivity of the results to differing assumptions. There is considerable sensitivity in fact, but it is not so extreme as to prevent the drawing of conclusions. This discussion of the methods of estimation appears in Chapter V.

To avoid burdening the ordinary reader with excessive detail, yet allow those interested to evaluate the particular data and methods used, some material has been put into two appendixes, one each for Chapters III and V. These may be omitted without loss of continuity and clarity.

The third section, contained in Chapter VI, is the main analytical part of the study. It is here that the results of the first two parts are combined in order to permit conclusions to be drawn about the impact of defense purchases on regional growth. The emphasis here is on quantitative results; the first two parts of the study—the model of growth, and the estimation of defense purchases by states—were explicitly designed to allow their integration in a quantitative way.

It was also possible, however, to construct the first two parts so that each could stand alone. The growth model, for example, can be used, in the form specified here, to analyze a host of other problems associated with regional growth, for it depends in no way upon the particular methods used to estimate the regional distribution of defense purchases. Furthermore, the estimates of purchases themselves are as suitable for use with other analytical models as they are with the one used here. Thus to the extent the methods of estimation are acceptable, the estimates themselves may stand alone.

Depending upon his interests, a reader may choose to read either Chapters III and IV, or Chapter V, if he desires. If he is interested only in general results, he may actually omit both of these parts and still glean something of value by reading Chapter VI, together with Chapter II, where a short summary of the methods of the first two parts is presented.

The fourth part of the study, contained in the final four chapters, is primarily descriptive rather than analytical. Chapters VII and VIII present a summary explanation of factors which underlie the changes in the regional distribution of each of the three components of defense purchases—procurement, military payrolls, and civilian employee payrolls. The explanation, it should be noted, includes no examination of the role of "politics" in determining the placement of contracts and installations. Rather, it describes in conventional terms the composition of the military bill of goods and the comparative advantages of regions. Although it would be naive to assume that political factors never play a role in these matters, I feel that popular discussion has overstated their influence, and that economic factors are generally sufficient to explain the important changes.

Chapter IX contains a brief discussion of the issues of defense purchases policy as related to regional distribution, including the question of whether contractors in "depressed" or "labor surplus" areas should be favored. Chapter X suggests some broad implications of the study's findings.

Technique of the Study

The study outlines and uses a simple model of regional growth, one in which the rate of growth of total personal income can be predicted by (but which does not equal) the rate of growth in a certain part of income, specified as "exogenous." Exogenous simply refers to that part of income which comes from "outside" a region, especially the income a region earns by selling goods and services (including the services of capital) to other regions. The study's estimates of defense purchases in each state are made on an annual basis and they are meant to represent total value added in production. For use with the personal income model in question, the amounts are scaled down to a personal income basis, called "defense income," for three representative years—1952, 1956, and 1962. All defense income is assumed to be part of exogenous income, and the expression of defense income as a percentage of total exogenous income is assumed to provide a measure of the relative dependence of a state or region on defense activity.

The reason for this latter assumption is that income from outside is viewed in this approach as the key element in the level and rate of growth of economic activity in a region. The local sector, consisting of the producers of goods for local use (by consumers, investors, or government), is seen as relatively passive—expanding if exogenous income grows, contracting if exogenous income falls. A gain of one dollar in exogenous income from defense or other demand means the gain of additional local income as well. The earners of income from outside respend the money received, and in so doing create demand for locally produced goods and services, causing the producers of those local goods to earn income as well. A dollar of income from outside thus supports more than a dollar of total income, because the original dollar earned is respent several times. Not all of this effect will be felt in the local sector, however, because some of the respending will be for goods imported into the region. But much of the effect will be felt locally. Therefore, outside or exogenous income has a multiplier effect, both when it increases and when it decreases.

Assume, for example, that in a particular year a state has a total of $4 billion in personal income. The methods used in this study, as detailed in Chapter III, may indicate that one-half of this amount, or $2 billion, is exogenous income; this is the amount the state's population receives from outside the state from exports, property, and transfer payments. The percentage used in this study to express relative dependence of a state or region on defense income is the ratio of defense income to exogenous income; if the estimate of defense income were $0.5 billion in the example, this figure would be 25 percent. It is a better measure of dependence on defense income than the ratio of defense income to total personal income—which would be only 12.5 percent—because it automatically takes into account the multiplier effects. For exogenous income as a whole, the multiplier in this example is 2; total personal income is twice exogenous income. If defense income has the same multiplier effects as other exogenous income, the total effect (original plus multiplier) of defense income is $1 billion, or 25 percent of total personal income. It should be obvious that the ratio of this total effect to personal income is the same as the ratio of defense income to exogenous income, as long as defense income is assumed to have the same multiplier effects as other exogenous income.

The relative importance of defense income, then, is best expressed as a fraction of the key sector only, not of total income. This same consideration suggests how to measure the impact of defense spending on *growth*. If the specification of exogenous income as the "key sector" is correct, any growth in a region's income depends on growth in its exogenous income. This is plausible, it is argued later, even if the *rate* of growth in total income happens to be higher than that in exogenous income. The approach used assumes that exogenous income initiates all growth, even though the rate of growth in the local sector paradoxically may be greater than in the exogenous sector itself. A way of measuring the relative contribution of defense income to growth in exogenous income is therefore a way of measuring the contribution of defense income to growth in general.

Over any given period, one way of measuring this contribution is by calculating the ratio of the growth rate for defense income to the growth rate for exogenous income as a whole, and then multiplying this ratio by the fractional weight of defense income in exogenous income in the initial year of the period. For example, assume defense income is 25 percent of total exogenous income at the beginning of a period, and that defense income grows at 4 percent and exogenous income at 5 percent over the period. The ratio of growth rates, .8, would be multiplied by the weight, .25, to give .20. This means that 20 percent of the growth in the period is contributed by defense income. Other measures are possible, of course, but this is the one used here. It will be noted that this measure is zero if defense income does not grow at all, no matter how important defense income is at the beginning of the period. It will be negative if defense income grows at a negative rate—that is, declines—while exogenous income grows. A negative "contribution" implies a depressing force which has to be overcome in order for any growth to take place at all.

Limitations of Results

It is impossible to stress too strongly that the results presented here are only estimates. They can be nothing else, for there are no data currently available which reveal what the regional distribution of defense purchases really is or has been in the past. There is no way to confirm the general accuracy of the estimates derived. Since they cannot be checked statistically, the reader must simply judge the reasonableness of the methods used to produce them. Further, of course, he must use with extreme care any of the hundreds of numbers derived from the estimating formulas. This state of affairs is most regrettable, but unavoidable. I have derived various alternative estimates at certain points, and noted the sensitivity of estimates to varying assumptions, but these precautions do little to improve the validity of the methods or the accuracy of the figures.

Even if the actual figures relevant to the regional distribution of defense spending were known, conceptual and statistical problems of measuring the impact on regional growth would remain. Many readers undoubtedly will object to the simple model used here. And some who accept the design and use of the model will object to the methods used to estimate exogenous income. Here, too, various alternatives have been used, but it was found, in the end, that all of the approaches served about equally well to explain the actual record of growth.

The many shortcomings of data and methods are discussed in the chapters which follow. Some readers may feel these are so serious as to render the estimates of little value. I would prefer to have more readers of this kind than of those who would rely upon the figures down to the last decimal place. For dubious readers, I hope the study is useful in pointing out some of the difficulties of research in this field, and that the initial efforts to deal with them will suggest methods of greater refinement.

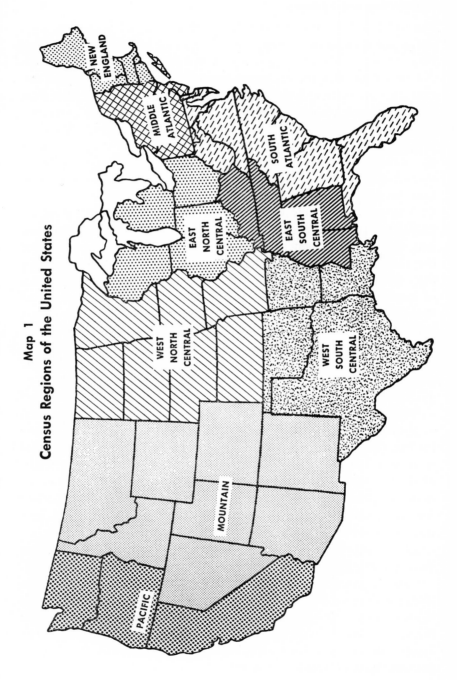

Map 1

Census Regions of the United States

General Summary of Results

This general summary gives some of the major results for the nine census regions in the United States. The results for each state are presented in the relevant chapters which follow. The figures for the large regions given below indicate the kinds of quantitative results derived but avoid the long tables of the later chapters which cover every state. Map 1 shows the boundaries of each region. It should be noted that the experience within a region may represent the aggregate of wide variations from state to state.

The growth model used here is one of the simplest types of regional base models. It predicts local income, and thus total income, as a linear function of exogenous income. The regression tests of the model, based upon annual observations for 1947-62, employ three different variants which differ according to the classification of industrial wages as export or local. Results of regressions for all three types are presented in Chapter IV. Since each of the variants works about equally well in predicting local income for most states, only two are retained as measures of exogenous income in later analysis; for most states, these two variants result in the highest and lowest levels of exogenous income. The variant omitted, of course, would usually have produced results between these two levels.

The states for which the model does not work well experienced large fluctuations in exogenous income, mainly farm income. Local income in these states remained much more stable than exogenous income, so a linear model produces poor fits. In such cases, a ratchet model (where the ratio of present income to previous peak income is an important explanatory variable) produces much better results. This fact implies that local income can still be well predicted by a linear function of exogenous income if exogenous income grows evenly, or if years with large fluctuations are omitted from the regressions.

The regression coefficients generally imply a multiplier for exogenous income of about 2.0; that is, an increase of one dollar in exogenous income roughly caused an increase of one dollar in local income, or two in total personal income. The size of the multiplier varied considerably both from state to state and also according to the definition of exogenous income. The estimates of the multiplier are of some interest in themselves, but they are not significant for later analysis. The regression tests were designed primarily to gauge the dependence of local income on exogenous income—to establish whether the relative importance of defense income in exogenous income could be an interesting and useful concept.

Before the model could be used to quantify the impact of defense income, estimates had to be made of the amounts of defense income itself which accrued to each state. This was accomplished in two steps, first by deriving defense purchases estimates, then by adjusting these amounts to the personal income basis required for use with the model. The purchases by state are estimates of the total value added at all stages of production in each state; they are of considerable interest in themselves, and they could be used for other purposes than as the bases for statements of income. Since the only data on the regional distribution of procurement are those for prime contracts, the estimation of procurement purchases depends heavily upon assumptions about the extent and geographical pattern of subcontracting and other purchases by prime contractors in one state from vendors in other states. Three alternative estimates of procurement by state were made, based upon three different assumptions about geographical patterns. The resulting estimates were found to be sensitive indeed to these assumptions, but not to the extent that valid conclusions could not be drawn. The three estimates were made in such a way that one is automatically the mean of the other two; this median estimate is the only one employed in later analysis. The high and low estimates are presented in the General Appendix; some readers may wish to make use of them by combining them with other figures given in the study.

Table 1 shows the median estimate of defense purchases for each region in 1952, 1956, and 1962, the representative years used for later analysis. These figures show the great shift in the regional distribution of defense production after the Korean War. The most dramatic shift, as noted above, was in the procurement category of purchases, but changes also occurred in military and civilian employee payrolls. These shifts benefitted New England and the southern and western parts of the country, at the expense of the Middle Atlantic and East North Central Regions.

Estimates of defense purchases were made for every year of the 1952-62 period. Defense income estimates were made in a simple

TABLE 1. Estimated Regional Defense Purchases in 1952, 1956, and 1962[a]

(Amounts in millions of dollars)

Region	1952 Amount	1952 Percent of U. S.	1956 Amount	1956 Percent of U. S.	1962 Amount	1962 Percent of U. S.
New England	2,944	7.36	2,668	7.97	3,698	8.27
Middle Atlantic	8,442	21.11	6,272	18.75	7,897	17.65
East North Central	9,660	24.16	5,571	16.65	6,705	14.99
West North Central	2,126	5.32	1,983	5.93	2,570	5.74
South Atlantic	5,295	13.24	5,012	14.98	6,762	15.11
East South Central	1,412	3.53	1,267	3.79	1,713	3.83
West South Central	2,702	6.76	2,722	8.14	3,335	7.45
Mountain	834	2.09	1,064	3.18	1,957	4.37
Pacific	6,305	15.77	6,508	19.45	9,535	21.31
United States	39,983	100.00	33,457	100.00	44,738	100.00

Source: Table 12.
[a] Regional amounts do not add to national totals because Alaska and Hawaii are not included in any region.

and crude form only for 1952, 1956, and 1962. (Readers may similarly adjust the purchase figures for any other year by following the method described in Chapter VI.)

The estimates of defense income expressed as percentages of exogenous income provide a measure of each region's relative dependence upon defense income. Calculations were made for each of the two measures of exogenous income, and these are presented in Chapter VI. Averages of the two percentages are shown in Table 2.

TABLE 2. Regional Defense Income as a Percentage of Exogenous Income, 1952, 1956, and 1962

Region	1952	1956	1962
New England	26.3	20.7	21.6
Middle Atlantic	25.8	16.4	15.5
East North Central	26.6	13.4	12.4
West North Central	14.9	13.6	12.5
South Atlantic	30.1	24.2	22.8
East South Central	20.7	16.8	16.4
West South Central	23.7	21.1	19.0
Mountain	17.6	19.3	22.6
Pacific	35.2	29.0	33.7

Source: Table 13.

These figures demonstrate how defense income varied in the three years in sustaining regional levels of personal income. The impact of defense income upon regional growth depends both upon the weight of defense income relative to total exogenous income and upon the rate of growth of defense income as well. Neither a high degree of dependence upon defense income nor a very rapid growth in defense income will alone contribute significantly to the general growth of a region. Both are necessary. As mentioned earlier, the weighted measure of the contribution of defense income to growth is the ratio of the growth rate in defense income to the

TABLE 3. Contribution of Defense Income to Regional Growth, 1952–62

(Percent of growth during period)

Region	1952–56	1956–62	1952–62
New England	−15	24	13
Middle Atlantic	−39	13	− 3
East North Central	−73	10	−21
West North Central	−17	10	8
South Atlantic	− 7	19	13
East South Central	−21	15	9
West South Central	1	13	11
Mountain	31	28	27
Pacific	2	28	21

Sources: Tables 14-16.

growth rate in exogenous income multiplied by the weight of defense income relative to total exogenous income in the initial year. This is only one of several such measures which could be calculated, especially if the initial year is used for the weight.

Table 3 shows rates of growth over the 1952-62 period and over two sub-periods, 1952-56 and 1956-62; here, too, the measures are averages of the two measures which correspond to the two different definitions of exogenous income.

In those periods and regions which experienced a decline, indicated by negative percentages, defense income contributed nothing positively to growth, and it actually was a depressing influence which had to be overcome for growth to take place at all. The majority of negative numbers for the 1952-56 period reflect widespread cutbacks after the Korean War. Three western regions, however, escaped cutbacks and in the Mountain Region defense income actually grew rapidly. The decline in this period affected the Middle Atlantic and East North Central Regions most seriously. From 1956 to 1962, defense income increased all over the country, but not uniformly. The same two regions which suffered the greatest losses in the first period received the smallest relative defense contribution to their growth in the second. The two westernmost regions gained large contributions, however, as did New England. For the entire ten-year period, the two westernmost regions experienced by far the largest favorable impact; in the Middle Atlantic and East North Central Regions, the recovery of defense income in the second period was not enough to offset the tremendous declines in the first, although the Middle Atlantic Region's recovery was nearly complete. It should be noted that in all regions, exogenous income did in fact grow at a positive rate in all three periods covered here. Incidentally, use of the initial year weight occasionally resulted in a rate of growth for the 1952-62 period which did not fall between the measures for the two sub-periods; the cumulative figure for the Mountain Region is an example of this.

These estimates indicate widely spread differential effects of the growth in defense demand. But defense demand was not the only force at work over the period. At the regional level, it appears that those regions which benefitted most from growth in defense income also tended to experience the fastest growth in total personal income, but this tendency was not very strong. As for growth in per capita income, there was very little observable relationship between the relative contribution of defense income to total income growth and the per capita growth actually achieved. This is shown in Table 4, column 1 of which is taken from Table 3.

A comparison of columns 1 and 2 in Table 4 shows a close rank agreement between growth in defense contributions and growth in personal income in each region. But since the regional differences in rate of growth of personal income are much smaller than are differences in defense contributions, the correlation between the two is rather weak. Defense contributions varied widely in the first four regions listed, for example, but differences in their rates of growth in personal income were slight. It is striking, however, that the two regions with the highest defense contributions also experienced the highest growth rates by far in personal income.

TABLE 4. Comparison of Defense Contribution and Regional Growth Actually Achieved, 1952–62

Region	Percent Defense Contribution, Entire Period (1)	Average Annual Percent Growth in Personal Income (2)	Average Annual Percent Growth in Per Capita Personal Income (3)
New England	13	4.8	3.4
Middle Atlantic	− 3	4.6	3.3
East North Central	−21	4.3	2.6
West North Central	8	4.5	3.5
South Atlantic	13	5.7	3.6
East South Central	9	4.7	4.0
West South Central	11	4.7	3.1
Mountain	27	6.3	2.7
Pacific	21	6.4	3.1

Sources: Table 16 and Office of Business Economics.

Agreement between columns 1 and 3 in Table 4 is far slighter, even in a ranking sense. The Mountain and Pacific Regions just referred to ranked seventh and eighth in per capita income growth. This suggests that the effect of defense income upon the increase in total level of activity in these regions was diluted by increases in population. What is notable here, though, is that the region with the lowest rate of growth in per capita income suffered the largest depressing effect from the shifts in defense demand.

The positive but weak relationship between defense contributions and rate of growth in personal income obtained not only regionally, but also at the state level. Furthermore, the lack of systematic agreement between defense contribution and per capita income growth is also evident at the state level.

No one can say what would have happened to a region had its share of defense purchases differed from that which it actually gained. Some areas would probably have found some other kind of export demand upon which to base growth. In other words, defense income might not have affected growth, but merely altered its character. On the other hand, some other areas surely would not have achieved so high a rate of growth had they been more dependent upon other kinds of production. Their comparative advantages simply seem to have been too limited. This study makes no attempt to consider these questions, but it seems reasonable to suggest that parts of the Middle Atlantic and East North Central Regions would have grown more rapidly had they experienced a higher level of defense purchases; the general excess capacity in these areas in the late 1950's suggests that increased defense income would have been a net addition, rather than merely a replacement of income from other sources. Parts of the Mountain Region and perhaps the Pacific Region seem to have received a clear net contribution from defense income. In these areas, as mentioned above, favorable influences stimulated both the growth in total economic activity and the increases in population.

CHAPTER II

Analytical Framework

THE MODEL USED HERE to describe economic growth in each state is one of a class known as regional base models. It is a personal income model in which some components of income are exogenous and others endogenous, so that in equilibrium, total income is a linear function of exogenous income. That is, exogenous income is "multiplied," just as in a national income model investment is multiplied, to determine total income. The quantitative significance of defense purchases is measured as a percentage of total exogenous income (purchases are first adjusted to a personal income basis). This allows the levels of significance to be compared among states and over time. The model is also designed to be useful for analyses of problems other than the regional impact of defense purchases. It is therefore specified and tested without reference to the proportion of exogenous income which derives from defense income. Defense income is analyzed in a separate procedure, which could be used to assess the significance of other parts of exogenous income as well.

The model is applied and tested through use of the extensive body of personal income and wage data available by state. Data are not uniformly published by state for a total value added or produced income concept. Exogenous income is assumed to be made up of wages and salaries in certain specific industries which are considered significant export industries in a given state, plus all property income and transfer payments. Three alternative approaches are made to the question of whether a given industry constitutes a significant source of export in a given state. These approaches produce a range of results, and alternative results are given in most of the applications of the model.

The model is used with annual observations of data for the period from 1947 to 1962.

Estimates of defense purchases by state are made consistent with the model; that is, purchases are measured on a personal income basis. Just as the model is designed to be useful in a general way, so the estimates of defense purchases themselves are fashioned to permit their use with other models. The estimates were derived in two steps: a value added series was constructed first, then the value added amounts were converted to a personal income basis. Value added figures for each year are presented in Table A-1; other researchers may find them useful with other models or for analysis of short-run fluctuations, which are not considered here.

The national totals of state estimates of value added are the total federal purchases of goods and services in the United States for the two budgetary categories, "military functions," and "foreign military assistance." There are three broad kinds of purchases: military wages and salaries, civilian wages and salaries, and procurement. Amounts for these in the postwar period are shown in Table 5. It is important to note that federal purchases for civilian space programs are *not* included in this study. These began to be significant about 1960, and amounted to $1.6 billion in 1962, the last year covered here.

The two wage and salary components present no great problems, since data by state are available from the Office of Business Economics. For procurement, however, only information about prime contracts by state is available, and this only from fiscal year 1951 on. The value of prime contracts awarded a state in a given year is not a satisfactory estimate of the value added in defense production in that state for two reasons: (1) a time lag occurs between the awarding of the contract and completion of production, so that some purchases under the contract are made in later years; (2) extensive subcontracting and other purchasing by prime contractors from vendors in other states means that value added is not equal to the total contract award (some of the contract value is produced

TABLE 5. Defense Purchases in the United States, 1947–62

(Millions of dollars)

Year	Military Wages and Salaries	Civilian Wages and Salaries	Procurement	Total
1947	2,901	2,060	. . .[a]	. . .[a]
1948	2,961	2,187	. . .[a]	. . .[a]
1949	3,212	2,333	. . .[a]	. . .[a]
1950	3,981	2,439	5,000	11,420
1951	6,785	3,883	18,000	28,668
1952	8,326	4,657	27,000	39,983
1953	8,212	4,622	29,400	42,234
1954	7,983	4,362	21,700	34,045
1955	7,789	4,613	19,700	32,102
1956	7,800	4,857	20,800	33,457
1957	7,694	4,952	24,000	36,646
1958	7,771	5,218	23,900	36,889
1959	8,024	5,520	25,500	39,044
1960	8,058	5,618	24,500	38,176
1961	8,187	5,922	27,100	41,209
1962	8,823	6,315	29,600	44,738

Sources: Military wages and salaries were taken from U. S. Office of Business Economics, *Personal Income by States since 1929,* a supplement to the *Survey of Current Business* (1956), and from articles on personal income by state (variously titled) in *Survey of Current Business,* Vols. 39–43 (August issues, 1959–63). The figures include pay of military personnel stationed in the United States plus allotments received by dependents residing in the United States from military personnel stationed abroad. Income in kind, consisting of food and standard clothing, is included. Amounts for Alaska are included only from 1950 on, for Hawaii in all years.

Civilian wages and salaries were derived partly from unpublished details of state personal income statistics furnished me by the Office of Business Economics, and partly from my own estimates. They represent earnings of civilians employed by the three military departments and the Office of the Secretary of Defense. Amounts for Alaska and Hawaii are included only from 1959 through 1962.

Procurement figures for 1952 through 1962 were taken from U. S. Office of Business Economics, *U. S. Income and Output,* a supplement to the *Survey of Current Business* (1958), Table III–9, and from "National Income and Product Accounts," *Survey of Current Business,* Vols. 42–43 (July issues, 1962–63), Table 27, and were adjusted by subtracting defense procurement abroad as estimated on the basis of data in the following articles: "Foreign Countries Earn $2.5 Billion from United States Military Outlays in 1953," *Survey of Current Business,* Vol. 34 (August 1954), pp. 7–8; "Defense Expenditures Abroad," *Survey of Current Business,* Vol. 39 (November 1959), pp. 15–17; and Cora E. Shepler, "United States Defense Expenditures Abroad," *Survey of Current Business,* Vol. 42 (January 1962), pp. 14–16. Figures for 1950 and 1951 were estimated on the basis of data for the wider category of purchases, "Major National Security." Amounts for Alaska and Hawaii are included in all years.

[a] Data insufficient to estimate either procurement or total.

elsewhere, and some value produced in the state is sold to prime contractors in other states).

An annual percentage share of total national value added was estimated for each state; these shares were then multiplied by the national total to obtain a dollar amount for each state. As noted earlier, this amount was eventually expressed as a percentage of total exogenous income for each state. A state's share of value added was estimated by: (1) applying a moving average to its annual prime contract shares, to adjust for time lag of purchases; (2) calculating a weighted average of the state's contract share (after the moving average was applied), its share of the national total of wages paid by a group of "defense-related" manufacturing industries, and its share of the national total of wages paid by all other manufacturing.

Such estimates were made for each of the calendar years 1951 to 1962. For three years—1952, 1956, and 1962—the value added estimates were translated into personal income terms by deducting the estimated amount of value added which does not become personal income, consisting chiefly of depreciation, corporate taxes, and retained earnings. For these years, defense income as a percentage of total exogenous income was calculated for each state. Exogenous income consists of wages and salaries in certain specific industries considered significant export industries for the state, plus all property income and transfer payments. The amount of defense income is a simple state total, not defined by industry; all defense income is assumed to be produced in export industries and thus included in total exogenous income. The percentages of exogenous income indicate the quantitative importance of defense income for each state, and, when used with relative growth rates, the contribution of defense income to growth.

CHAPTER III

A Simple Model of
Regional Growth

Several general characteristics of the model of regional growth should be pointed out before it is formally described. First, it is a model of growth over a period of intermediate length, specifically the post-World War II years, 1947 to 1962. Second, it is concerned with income rather than employment or some other macroeconomic variable, and it focuses upon the demand side of income determination without considering growth in capacity. Third, it classifies as either exogenous or endogenous each income component for which regional data are available. Finally, it is a partial model applied separately to individual states, rather than one which simultaneously explains growth in several states.

Income is the single most important variable a regional model should attempt to "explain" or predict, for it has the important advantage of breadth as a measure of economic activity and of comparability among regions. This book considers only growth in current dollar income; since trends in prices differ only slightly from region to region within the United States, relative growth in a region's money income is indicative of the relative growth of that region's real income.[1]

Although constraints on capacity are important, mobility of factors makes capacity in any one region more elastic than national capacity. In any case, since regional data on capacity are not generally available, a pure demand model is far simpler to implement than would be one which also attempts to account for changes in capacity.

Regional income statistics compiled in the United States are designed to reveal *personal income,* rather than a "gross regional product" or "regional income at factor cost." Personal income is geographically classified according to where it is received, not where earned. Fortunately, a large part of personal income—wages and salaries—is received mostly where earned; detailed industrial classification is also available for this portion of income.

Personal income and wage and salary data are published mainly for states; few complete and consistent series exist for smaller areas. This limitation virtually dictates the use of states, and regions made up of an integral number of states, as basic units for any discussion of regional income developments all over the nation.

The Office of Business Economics issues personal income totals for each year, and subtotals for these components:[2]

Wages and Salaries
Other Labor Income
Proprietors' Income, Farm and Nonfarm separately
Property Income
Transfer Payments
Personal Contributions for Social Insurance (negative)

[1] U. S. Office of Business Economics, *Personal Income by States* (1956), p. 10; Abner Hurwitz and Carlyle P. Stallings, "Interregional Differentials in Per Capita Real Income Change," in National Bureau of Economic Research, *Regional Income,* Vol. XXI of *Studies in Income and Wealth* (Princeton, 1957), pp. 195-265.

[2] Data for 1929-55 may be found in U. S. Office of Business Economics, *Personal Income by States since 1929,* a supplement to the *Survey of Current Business* (1956). Data for subsequent years have been published annually in the August issues of the *Survey of Current Business. Personal Income by States since 1929* describes in great detail the principles and estimating methods used. See also Edwin F. Terry, "Regional Income Account Estimates," in *Elements of Regional Accounts,* Werner Z. Hirsch (ed.), (Johns Hopkins, 1964), pp. 25-43, for comments on the Office of Business Economics methods.

The Wages and Salaries portion is further subdivided by industry. Some subgroups correspond to one-digit industries in the Standard Industrial Classification; others correspond to two-digit industries. The chief shortcoming of this breakdown is that there is no industrial detail within the manufacturing sector. Except in a few selected years, for which data on two-digit industries are given, only a single total figure is provided for manufacturing wages in each state. Fortunately for the purpose at hand, Bureau of Employment Security data contain finer industrial detail on total wages earned by employees covered by the unemployment insurance programs for each year from 1947 through 1962.[3] The BES figures cover at least 90 percent of all wages in mining, manufacturing, and large scale enterprise in some other industries, and they are subdivided into two-digit SIC industries, with additional data (since 1950) for some three-digit industries.

A blended industrial breakdown of state personal income components was devised from the statistics of the Office of Business Economics and those of the Bureau of Employment Security. Where coverage of the BES data was adequate, its finer divisions were used; in industries where BES coverage was not adequate, the broader groupings of the Office of Business Economics had to be used. The composite classification was constructed in such a way that no industry's wages are duplicated in another's.

Each of the resulting components of income was then designated either exogenous or endogenous for each state. This division is the most important aspect of the model. Such a division is in accord with the standard theory of aggregate income determination, but it is not the same as consumption versus investment and government purchases. When states are used as the basis for reporting of personal income, much of that income will be generated endogenously in local activity and trade. On the other hand, since states are tightly interrelated in the national economy, developments outside a given state will significantly affect its *exports* to other states.

[3] U. S. Bureau of Employment Security, *Employment and Wages of Workers Covered by State Unemployment Insurance Laws* (Office of Program Review and Analysis, annually 1947-49, quarterly 1950-62). The appendix to this chapter examines two reporting changes, one in 1956 and one in 1958, which cause breaks in continuity of these data. The breaks are not serious enough to warrant a change in any major conclusion of this study. The Office of Business Economics personal income data are free from such reporting changes.

A model of *simultaneous* income determination in the states is obviously desirable, but data on interregional trade do not exist in enough detail to allow implementation of such a model on the state level. One form of the simultaneous model, however, serves as a starting point:

$$(1) \quad Y_i = u_i(Y_i) - m_i(Y_i) + A_i + \sum_{j=1,\ j \neq i}^{n} m_{ij}(Y_j), \quad i = 1, \cdots, n,$$

where: i denotes region; Y_i is income in region i; $u_i(Y_i)$ is a function relating certain kinds of expenditure to income in region i; $m_i(Y_i)$ is a function relating imports by region i to its income; A_i is expenditure in region i which is independent of income in region i and of income in any other region; and $m_{ij}(Y_j)$ is a function relating exports from region i to region j (imports by region j from region i) to income in region j.

This model explains the level of income in a region by autonomous expenditure in the region, income earned by exporting to other regions, and expenditure and import functions; the expenditure function determines the multiplier of autonomous and export expenditure, subject to leakages from imports. The $u_i(Y_i)$ function may include induced investment as well as consumption.

The model, which was proposed by Metzler,[4] resembles an input-output model if linear functions are specified, but differs from an input-output model because it employs income variables instead of shipments, and regions instead of industries. With known parameters and autonomous expenditures, the model can be solved for the equilibrium income of each of the n regions. Since data are not available for this solution, a conceptual alternative is to estimate the parameters statistically, given estimates of A and Y for past periods. This procedure would require deriving reduced forms, estimating their parameters by least squares, then solving for structural parameters. If each region is allowed to have some direct or indirect trading connections with all other regions, each reduced form would have n predetermined variables (all n series for A). In order to preserve many degrees of freedom, either a small number of regions or many observations are required.[5]

[4] Lloyd A. Metzler, "A Multiple-Region Theory of Income and Trade," *Econometrica,* Vol. 18 (October 1950), pp. 329-54.

[5] The precise estimation of even the reduced-form parameters may be difficult because of collinearity of the A's.

The model used here sacrifices simultaneous determination yet recognizes dependence of a state on the *rest of the nation as a whole*. It is essentially an adaptation of the simple national income model. Consider the following equations, which apply to a *single* state in a given year:

(2) $$Y_h = h(Y_p),$$

(3) $$Y_p = Y_h + P + E,$$

where: Y_p is personal income; Y_h is wages and salaries and propri-etors' income in "local" industries, dependent only on total personal income; P is the sum of property income and transfer payments, both considered exogenous; and E is wages and salaries and proprietors' income in industries, including export industries, for which demand is exogenous.

Each state's income can be described with such a model, which is a member of the regional base family because it specifies that at least part of the exogenous sector is made up of export industries. Unlike some regional base models which use employment rather than income as the significant variable, and which include *only* ex-port activity in the exogenous sector, the above model includes property income and transfer payments. These two forms of income are not considered at all if employment is the variable used. It should also be noted that regional base theory is usually applied to cities or metropolitan areas, rather than to regions as large as states.

Defense purchases are assumed here to be part of exports from the state to the rest of the nation. Wages and salaries generated by defense demand are included in E; interest and dividends in P. Like other exogenous income, defense income is "multiplied." As presented here, the model treats E as a single total, without distinguishing the defense and non-defense parts; only later, in applying the model, is the distinction made. It is helpful to think of $h(Y_p)$ as $u(Y_p) - m(Y_p)$, where u is a total spending function and m an import function, both in terms of generated wages and proprietors' income. The h function, that is, applies to spending after import leakage is deducted. In linear form:

(4) $$Y_h = a + hY_p,$$

(5) $$Y_p = Y_h + P + E;$$

FIGURE 1. Equilibrium Level of Personal Income According to the Theory of Equations (4) through (7)

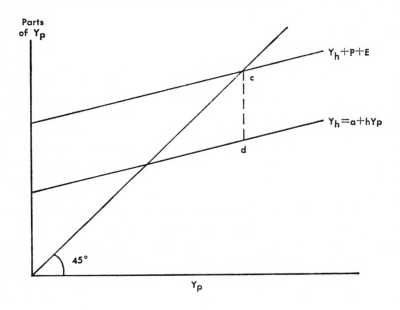

so that:

(6)
$$Y_p = \frac{a}{1-h} + \frac{(P+E)}{1-h},$$

(7)
$$Y_h = \frac{a}{1-h} + \frac{h}{1-h}(P+E).$$

Figure 1 shows the equilibrium level of personal income according to the theory of equations (4) through (7). This diagram is strictly analogous to the one commonly used to show the equilibrium aggregate income in the usual model incorporating an exogenous level of investment and a linear consumption function. In Figure 1, either of the two coordinates of c shows the equilibrium level of personal income as predicted by equation (6); at that point, the ordinate of point d shows the level of Y_h. Figure 1 is drawn with a positive value for a. Since present application of the model does not envisage situations where $(P+E)$ is zero, it is not necessary to speculate on the level of Y_h at that point. The important thing is that the experience of a state may be such that a straight line through actually observed $Y_h - Y_p$ points could have either a zero, positive, or negative intercept *if* extended to the vertical axis. The sign of a has important implications for the rate of growth of Y_h relative to the rate of growth of $(P + E)$.

Whether industries are in E or in Y_h depends on whether the demand to which they respond is considered exogenous. In this study three different bases of classification are used and tested. These are described in detail below, but for the moment it should be noted that all three classifications cut across the usual distinction between consumption and investment by specifying that not all investment goods industries are considered exogenous, and that consumer goods industries producing for export are exogenous.

In this study only the linear form of the model, and a "ratchet," or ratio-to-previous-peak form, are used. Use of linear relationships is essentially an initial exploration. The $h(Y_p)$ function is the sum of three functions for consumption, induced investment, and imports. A sufficient but not necessary condition for a linear sum is that each of these functions be linear. Since linear consumption and import functions are common in such initial efforts, more justification for their use is not attempted here. Reliance on linear forms would definitely not be justified if the model were used to describe cyclical movements, but here the emphasis is on long-run growth. A linear investment function would be consistent with the linear accelerator theory if income grew at a constant rate. Since Y_h is in terms of wages, an additional assumption—that local wages are a linear function of local expenditure—may be added. These assumptions are sufficient but not strictly necessary, since some nonlinearities may offset others.

Rates of Growth

Rates of growth of both Y_p and Y_h can be derived from equations (6) and (7). In the continuous variable case, if dotted variables represent time derivatives:

$$Y_p = \frac{1}{1-h} (P + E).$$

If $A = P + E$, and $\dfrac{\dot{Y}_p}{Y_p}$ is the rate of growth in Y_p:

$$\frac{\dot{Y}_p}{Y_p} = \frac{1}{1-h} \frac{\dot{A}}{Y_p} \frac{A}{A}$$

$$= \frac{1}{1-h} \frac{A}{A} \frac{A}{Y_p}$$

$$= \frac{1}{1-h} \frac{\dot{A}}{A} \frac{A}{a+A}; $$
$$\qquad\qquad\qquad\qquad \overline{1-h}$$

(8) $$\frac{Y_p}{Y_p} = \frac{\dot{A}}{A} \frac{A}{a+A}.$$

Similarly for Y_h:

$$\frac{\dot{Y}_h}{Y_h} = \frac{h}{1-h} \frac{\dot{A}}{A} \frac{A}{Y_h}$$

$$= \frac{h}{1-h} \frac{\dot{A}}{A} \frac{A}{a+hA}; $$
$$\qquad\qquad\qquad\qquad \overline{1-h}$$

(9) $$\frac{\dot{Y}_h}{Y_h} = \frac{\dot{A}}{A} \frac{hA}{a+hA}.$$

The sign and value of a are important. If a is zero, both Y_p and Y_h grow at the same rate as exogenous income. If a is positive and if $\dot{Y}$ is positive, both Y_p and Y_h grow more slowly than A; if a is negative, Y_p and Y_h grow faster than the exogenous sector.

For the discrete case, and using an average geometric rate of growth over a period, results are as follows. If r_p, r_h, and r_A are the rates of growth for Y_p, Y_h, and A, respectively, and subscript o denotes the first year of the period:

$$(1+r_p)^t = \frac{Y_{pt}}{Y_{po}} = \frac{1}{Y_{po}} \frac{1}{1-h} (a+A_t)$$

$$= \frac{1}{Y_{po}} \frac{1}{1-h} [a + A_o(1+r_A)^t]$$

$$= \frac{1}{a+A_o} \frac{1}{1-h} [a + A_o(1+r_A)^t];$$
$$\qquad\quad \overline{1-h}$$

$$(10) \qquad (1 + r_p)^t = \frac{a + A_{\bullet}(1 + r_A)^t}{a + A_{\bullet}} \,.$$

Similarly, for Y_h:

$$(1 + r_h)^t = \frac{Y_{ht}}{Y_{h\bullet}} = \frac{1}{Y_{h\bullet}} \left[\frac{a}{1-h} + \frac{h}{1-h} A_t \right]$$

$$= \frac{1}{Y_{h\bullet}} \frac{1}{1-h} \left[a + h A_{\bullet}(1 + r_A)^t \right]$$

$$= \frac{1}{\dfrac{a + hA_{\bullet}}{1-h}} \frac{1}{1-h} \left[a + h A_{\bullet}(1 + r_A)^t \right];$$

$$(11) \qquad (1 + r_h)^t = \frac{a + h A_{\bullet}(1 + r_A)^t}{a + h A_{\bullet}} \,.$$

The preceding remarks about the sign and value of a apply to the discrete case as well.

The growth of a region described by this model can be relatively rapid if exogenous income is growing rapidly and/or if a is negative and large in absolute value. A region may have a favorable composition of exports—that is, its industries may be growing rapidly throughout the nation; or, within industries, growth may be more rapid in one region than in others. A negative value for a means that the multiplier response at the margin is greater than the accumulated responses of the past which determined the value of Y_h/Y_p at the beginning of the period.

Aside from changing habits of consumption, three explanations of a higher marginal response are possible: (1) Induced investment may occur partly in the local sector; for example, as described in detail later, the model as used here includes all of construction in Y_h. Induced investment may be stronger in the postwar period than previously, or it may be progressively increasing in strength—in effect shifting the parameter h above the value of Y_h/Y_p. The strength of induced investment depends on marginal capital requirements and on what share of them local industries can meet. (2) If state and local government salaries are included in Y_h, as they are here, a higher than proportional increase in government spending in response to rising income will result in a higher marginal response. (3) A region may spend relatively more and more of its income on domestic goods by replacing imports. This reduces import "leakage." Several factors could work through all three of these processes. One is population growth. If an increase in population accompanies an increase in income, the response of induced investment and of state and local government may be stronger than if income alone increases, and increasing size of markets may allow import replacement. These effects would occur even if variables are measured per capita. A second factor, accelerated urbanization, would have a similar effect. Specifically, migration may produce more favorable effects than natural increase in population because housing requirements may be greater, and because adult immigrants may widen the market more than would newborn children. Third, the composition of E significantly affects induced investment; growth in completely new industries may have greater marginal requirements than expansion of established ones, though such growth may be offset by a rise in import requirements.

These effects could perhaps be distinguished by disaggregating the local and exogenous sectors and estimating separate parameters, then by comparing regional differences in the parameters to differences in rate of population growth, rate of urbanization, types of export industries, and so forth. This procedure is beyond the scope of the present study.

Implementing the Model

The model was tested in its linear form by using annual data by state for the 1947-62 period, with per capita variables. The test employed three different variants of A, exogenous income (thus giving rise to three corresponding variants of Y_h, endogenous income, as well, since Y_h is defined as total personal income minus exogenous income). Each variant of A includes property income and transfer payments, the sum of which is P. The classification of these two factors as exogenous is discussed further in the appendix to this chapter. The three variants of A differ according to three definitions of E, income from exports outside the state or region. They will be identified in the rest of the book by E_1, E_2, and E_3, as defined below.

E_1, which when added to P gives A_1, consists of wages and salaries (but not proprietors' income) earned in all mining, manufacturing, and what the personal income statistics call "other industries," a small miscellaneous category; all wages and proprietors' income earned in agriculture; and all federal government payrolls, both civilian and military. Corresponding to this definition, Y_{h1} includes all the rest of personal income, namely wages and salaries in all other industries besides mining, manufacturing, and "other industries;" "other labor income," which is chiefly employers' contributions to private pension and welfare plans for employees; nonfarm proprietors' income; and, as a negative item, personal contributions for social insurance.

E_2, which when added to P gives A_2, includes agricultural income and federal payrolls, and the wages in the "other industries," just as does E_1. E_2 differs from E_1, however, in that it does *not* include *all* manufacturing and mining, and *does* include some industries outside manufacturing and mining. The difference lies in the fact that the additional industries included in a state's E_2, and which distinguish it from E_1, are only those considered to have *significant export demand*—that is, export outside the state or region. Such industries are included in their *entirety* under the definition of E_2.

Two industries were identified *a priori* as significant export industries for all states: SIC 19, Ordnance, and SIC 37, Transportation Equipment. For all other judgments, the location coefficient criterion was applied. The location coefficient for a particular state and industry is defined as:

$$\frac{\left(\dfrac{\text{Wages in the industry in the state}}{\text{Wages in the industry in the nation}} \right)}{\left(\dfrac{\text{Wages in all industries in the state}}{\text{Wages in all industries in the nation}^{6}} \right)},$$

which expresses the importance of an industry in a state relative to the importance of that industry in the nation as a whole. A coefficient above 1.0 in value is usually viewed as evidence that the industry in question is producing, at least in part, for export outside the state.

---

[6] Walter Isard, *Methods of Regional Analysis* (Technology Press of the Massachusetts Institute of Technology, 1960), p. 123.

This test is only a rough guide, and there are many difficulties in its use.[7] Variations in taste and in capital-labor ratios from state to state can produce coefficients above 1.0 even for exclusively local industries, and below 1.0 even for industries with a significant export demand. At the level of aggregation in the data, *every* industry in fact produces both for export and for local demand. Finally, since only partial coverage of wages is available for some industries which are neither mining nor manufacturing, the coefficient can be distorted if coverage in a state is different from that in the whole nation.

In classifying industries in E_2 in this study, the effect of some of these shortcomings has been reduced in the following ways: First, to allow for variations in taste, production functions, and data coverage, the critical value was set at 1.2, rather than 1.0.[8] This variation is especially important, because if an industry qualifies at all, its entire wages are included in E_2. Coefficients were calculated for both 1947 and 1962; if the value was 1.2 or more in either year, the industry was included. Second, many industries for which varying tastes and data coverage are crucial were identified *a priori* as *endogenous,* and for these, the location coefficient criterion was not relied upon. Briefly, these industries consisted of state and local government, construction, and most services; they are discussed in greater detail in the appendix to this chapter.

The third variant of the export sector is E_3, which when added to P gives A_3, the third variant of total exogenous income. E_3 was derived by adjusting E_2 to eliminate wages due to the large "local" production which takes place even in an industry with significant export demand. The adjustments were carried out as follows: Except for SIC 19 and SIC 37, estimated wages earned in response to local demand were eliminated for all industries included in E_3 under the location coefficient criterion. This was done crudely but consistently by subtracting an amount large enough to leave only the amount which caused the location coefficient to be above 1.0 in value. For instance, if for a particular year in a particular

[7] *Ibid.,* pp. 123 ff.

[8] A critical value above 1.0, as well as *a priori* judgments, were also used in a regional base study by George Hildebrand and Arthur Mace, Jr., "The Employment Multiplier in an Expanding Industrial Market: Los Angeles County, 1940-1947," *Review of Economics and Statistics,* Vol. 32 (August 1950), pp. 241-49.

state the location coefficient for an industry was 1.5, it was assumed that two-thirds (1.0/1.5) of the industry's wages were earned in local production and one-third (.5/1.5) in export production, and only the latter fraction was included in the export sector. If the coefficient was 2.5, only 60 percent (1.5/2.5) of the industry was included in the export sector, and so on. Reductions were carried out for each state in each of the sixteen years covered by the study.[9]

This adjustment was not carried out for SIC 19, since all of it was assumed to be an export industry. Likewise, within SIC 37, the adjustment was carried out only for the sub-industry SIC 371, Motor Vehicles; the rest of SIC 37 (SIC 372, Aircraft; 373, Ships and Boats; 374, Railroad Equipment; and 375, Motorcycles and Bicycles) was assumed to be wholly export-oriented. Since three-digit industry data by state are not available for all years before 1950, this adjustment required some estimation, by extrapolation, of SIC 371 wages for that period. If the coefficient for SIC 371 was less than 1.0, this sub-industry was given a value of zero in E_3.

It should also be noted that no such adjustment was made for agricultural income, federal payrolls, and wages in "other industries;" all of these amounts were assumed to represent export income.

Such adjustment procedures are crude, and there are even more objections to use of the location coefficient in this manner in determining an exact fraction for export demand, than to its use in identifying industries with "significant" export demand. Nevertheless, in the absence of extensive sample surveys of firms in all states, it is the best approach for purposes of the broad analysis carried out here.[10]

Table 6 lists the export industries for each state which are in-

[9] Two minor points should be mentioned. Industries were included in E_2 in the first place only if their coefficient in either 1947 or 1962 was higher than 1.2. But the adjustment for E_3 left all the wages which were responsible for a coefficient greater than 1.0. An industry may have had a coefficient above 1.2 for several years in the period, but one below 1.2 at other times. In that case, the whole industry was included for every year in E_2, and part of the industry was included in E_3 for every year in which the coefficient was 1.0 or larger. If the coefficient fell below 1.0, the industry was given a zero value in calculating E_3 for that year. Note also that if an industry had a location coefficient *between* 1.0 and 1.2 during the period, it was included in *neither* E_2 nor E_3.

[10] Such extensive sample surveys have been undertaken for some areas. See, for example, W. Lee Hansen and Charles M. Tiebout, "An Intersectoral Flows Analysis of the California Economy," *Review of Economics and Statistics,* Vol.

cluded in E_2 and E_3. It shows that most of the export industries as classified here are mining, manufacturing, or transportation. Finance and tourist-oriented industries are included for some states, and there are a few other scattered exceptions to the general rule.

To return to E_1 for a moment, it is difficult to defend, *a priori,* as a definition of the export sector, but quite simple to compute from the official statistics (compared with the computations of E_2 and E_3, which were burdensome, requiring thousands of location coefficients and the adding of quarterly amounts to get annual totals in the case of the BES data) and thus rather easy to test. E_1 probably overstates the export sector for most states, since so much manufacturing and mining is really for local consumption or investment. While the E_1 definition also errs in the opposite direction, in not including export industries outside manufacturing and mining, this is probably not enough to offset the first kind of error. For almost every state in the period analyzed, E_1 is somewhat larger than E_2 and thus larger than E_3.

An attempt to choose between E_2 and E_3 intuitively, on the other hand, is more difficult. Conceptually, E_3 is preferable, but the crudeness of the location coefficient method of allocation clouds the issue. While E_3 may appear to have the more nearly correct magnitude, it is not clearly possible to say which definition shows a rate of growth closer to the true rate of growth of export income. The uncertainty is all the greater because of the high degree of aggregation in the data. Application of the location coefficient method to a two-digit industry may show that that industry has little export demand, but this procedure ignores the possibility that within the two-digit industry there may be one or more three-digit industries which produce primarily for export. Such industries are particularly likely to be hidden within SIC 33, Primary Metals; SIC 35, Nonelectrical Machinery; and SIC 39, Miscellaneous Manufacturing.

The three variants of Y_h are simply total personal income minus the corresponding variant of A; for example, Y_{h1} is $Y_p - A_1$, and so on. Since some export wages are taken from the covered wages data of the BES, they exclude small amounts of uncovered wages in the industry. These amounts *are* included in total personal income by the OBE, so deriving Y_h by subtraction means they are included in Y_h. They are earned mostly in very small establishments, so they

---

45 (November 1963), pp. 409-18; and Bruce F. Duncombe, *Upper Midwest Commodity Flows, 1958* (Upper Midwest Economic Study, 1962).

TABLE 6. Composition of the Export Sector of the Model for States and Regions[a]

State or Region	Mining	Manufacturing	Finance	Transportation	Other
Maine		19, 22, 24, 26, 31, 37			Hotels
New Hampshire		19, 22, 24–26, 31, 35–37			Hotels
Vermont	All but fuels	19, 22, 24–26, 32, 35, 37, 39		Railroads	Hotels
Massachusetts		19, 22, 23, 26, 27, 30, 31, 35–39	63		80
Connecticut		19, 22, 30, 33–39	63		
Rhode Island		19, 22, 30, 34–39			
New England		19, 22, 30, 31, 34–39	63		
New York		19, 23, 27, 31, 36–39	All finance	"Other"	Communications, Hotels, Amusement and recreation, 73, 81, 86
New Jersey		19, 22, 23, 28–30, 32, 36–39	63	44	
Pennsylvania	Coal	19, 21–23, 29, 31–34, 36–38		Railroads	
Middle Atlantic	Anthracite coal	19, 21, 23, 27, 28, 33, 36–39	All finance	"Other"	73, 79, 81
Ohio		19, 30, 32–37			
Indiana	14	19, 25, 29, 30, 32–37			
Illinois		19, 20, 25, 27, 34–39		Railroads, Highway	
Michigan	10	19, 25, 30, 33–35			
Wisconsin		19, 20, 25, 26, 31, 34–38			
East North Central		19, 25, 26, 30, 33–37			
Minnesota	10	19, 20, 26, 32, 37, 38		Railroads	80
Iowa	14	19, 20, 35, 37			
Missouri	10	19, 20, 23, 31, 32, 37		Railroads, Highway	
North Dakota	13	19, 37		Railroads	
South Dakota	All but fuels	19, 20, 37			
Nebraska		19, 20, 37	63	Railroads	
Kansas	Petroleum, 14	19, 20, 29, 37		Railroads	Public utilities
West North Central	10	19, 20, 31, 37		Railroads	
Delaware		19, 23, 28, 30, 31, 37	Banking	"Other"	
Maryland		19, 33, 37		"Other"	
District of Columbia		19, 27, 37			Hotels, 81, 86
Virginia	Coal	19, 21, 22, 25, 28, 37		Railroads, "Other"	
West Virginia	Coal, 14	19, 28, 32, 33, 37		Railroads	Public utilities
North Carolina		19, 21, 22, 24, 25, 36, 37		Highway	
South Carolina		19, 21–24, 26, 28, 37			
Georgia	14	19, 22–24, 26, 37		Railroads	
Florida	14	19, 21, 37		"Other"	Hotels, 79
South Atlantic	Coal, 14	19, 21, 22, 24, 25, 28, 37			Hotels
Kentucky	Coal, 14	19, 21, 37		Railroads	
Tennessee	14	19, 22–25, 28, 30, 31, 37			
Alabama	Coal, 10	19, 22–24, 26, 30, 33, 37		"Other"	
Mississippi	Petroleum	19, 23–26, 37			
East South Central	All but coal	19, 21–25, 28, 37		Railroads	
Arkansas	All but coal	19, 24–26, 29, 31, 37		Railroads	
Oklahoma	Petroleum	19, 29, 37		"Other"	
Louisiana	Petroleum, 14	19, 24, 26, 28, 29, 37		"Other"	Public utilities
Texas	Petroleum, 14	19, 28, 29, 37		"Other"	Public utilities
West South Central	Petroleum, 14	19, 24, 29, 37		"Other"	Public utilities

34

TABLE 6—Continued

State or Region	Mining	Manufacturing	Finance	Transportation	Other
Montana	All but coal	19, 24, 29, 33, 37		Railroads	Hotels
Idaho	10	19, 20, 24, 28, 37		Railroads	
Wyoming	All mining	19, 29, 37		Railroads	Hotels
Colorado	Petroleum, 10	19, 30, 37		Highway	Hotels
Utah	All mining	19, 29, 33, 37		Railroads	
Nevada	10,14	19, 37		Railroads	Hotels, 79, 81
Arizona	10	19, 36, 37			Hotels, Public utilities
New Mexico	All but coal	19, 37		Railroads	Hotels, Public utilities
Mountain	All mining	19, 24, 37		Railroads	Hotels, 79
Washington		19, 24, 26, 33, 37		"Other"	
Oregon		19, 24, 26, 37		Railroads, Highway, 44	
California	Petroleum	19, 24, 29, 36, 37		"Other"	Amusement and recreation
Pacific		19, 24, 29, 37		"Other"	Amusement and recreation
Hawaii		19, 20, 37		"Other"	Hotels, 79
Alaska	Petroleum, 10	19, 20, 24, 37		"Other"	Hotels, Communications

Source: Office of Business Economics and Bureau of Employment Security.

ᵃ In addition to agriculture, federal government, and the miscellaneous small "other industries" referred to in the text, the industries in this table comprise the E_2 and E_3 sectors for each state and region. Numbers refer to SIC industries, explained below; words refer to titles of industries used in the personal income statistics of the Office of Business Economics.

Key to Standard Industrial Classification (SIC) industries:

Mining
10 Metal Mining
14 Nonmetallic Mining and Quarrying, except Fuels

Manufacturing
19 Ordnance and Accessories
20 Food and Kindred Products
21 Tobacco Manufactures
22 Textile Mill Products
23 Apparel
24 Lumber and Wood Products, except Furniture
25 Furniture and Fixtures
26 Paper and Allied Products
27 Printing, Publishing, and Allied Industries
28 Chemicals and Allied Products
29 Petroleum Refining
30 Rubber and Miscellaneous Plastics
31 Leather Products
32 Stone, Clay, and Glass Products
33 Primary Metals
34 Fabricated Metal Products
35 Nonelectrical Machinery
36 Electrical Machinery and Equipment
37 Transportation Equipment
38 Instruments, Photographic, Optical, and Timekeeping Equipment
39 Miscellaneous Manufacturing

Transportation
44 Water Transportation

Finance
63 Insurance Carriers

Other
73 Miscellaneous Business Services (advertising, building services, credit and collection services, and others)
79 Amusement and Recreation other than Motion Pictures
80 Medical and Health Services
81 Legal Services
86 Nonprofit Membership Organizations

can be assumed to depend on local demand even though larger establishments in the industry are more nearly export-oriented. Unfortunately, some small firms are covered by the BES data only for
part of the 1947-62 period. This distortion, which seems very
small, is discussed in the appendix to this chapter.

For purposes of defining the export sector, the nine multi-state
regions (Census divisions) used in this study are treated exactly as
are states. The export sectors under the E_2 and E_3 definitions are
not, therefore, the mere sums of the corresponding sectors in the
region's states. The location coefficient criterion was applied to the
region as a whole. An industry may be included for some of a region's states, but not for the region itself, because it exports out of
one state and into another within the region. There are generally
fewer industries in a regional export sector than in some of the
states within the region. It is also true that some industries included
in a region's export sector are not included in the export sectors of
all the region's member states, under the E_2 and E_3 definitions. (The
E_1 definition for a region *is* the sum of the export sectors for the region's states.)

The simple model can be tested by fitting equations (6) and (7)
by least squares. Proper estimation procedure calls for estimation of
equations (6) and (7) rather than equation (4), to avoid the simultaneous equation problem.[11] However, the least squares estimate of
$1/(1 - h)$ in equation (6) is always equal to one plus the estimate of
$h/(1 - h)$ in equation (7). The two equations give identical estimates
of $a/(1 - h)$. Therefore, only one equation need be fitted. With
respect to the correlation coefficient, use of equation (6) may be ob-
jected to because Y_p is being regressed on a large part of itself.
Therefore, equation (7) was the one fitted for each state and region.
Annual data for the period 1947 through 1962 were used, except
for Alaska, for which personal income data are unavailable before
1950. (The personal income data are available only annually, although the BES data on wages are reported on a quarterly basis.)
The results of the regressions are discussed in the following chapter.

[11] See, for example, Trygve Haavelmo, "Methods of Measuring the Marginal
Propensity to Consume," *Journal of the American Statistical Association,* Vol.
42 (March 1947), pp. 105-22; reprinted in William Hood and Tjalling Koopmans (eds.), *Studies in Econometric Method* (Wiley, 1953).

Appendix to Chapter III

SOME COMPONENTS of personal income were classified *a priori* as exogenous under all three definitions. Similarly, other components were considered endogenous or local *a priori*.

A Priori *Exogenous Income*

Transfer payments and property income, which fall into this category, are largely determined by forces outside the state where received. Social security, veterans and personnel pensions, and other federal payments are the most important stable transfer payments. Widespread changes of residence by retired persons are one reason for considering these exogenous; federal origin of the payments is another. Unemployment benefits are closely related to cyclical movements, especially those associated with a region's export industries, which show the greatest decline and unemployment in recession.

The failure of the data to disaggregate property income within states, however, raises a difficult question about that component. Some parts of it clearly should be endogenous. Large amounts represent imputed interest and rents (of owner-occupied nonfarm dwellings) and monetary rents, all of which are probably rather dependent on total personal income. On the other hand, monetary interest and dividends together comprise the larger part of property income, and these are largely exogenous to a state. Since information is not available on the state distribution of any part except the grand total, all of it was included in the exogenous sector.

Certain earned income components were also considered to be *a priori* exogenous income. Among these, all farm wages and farm proprietors' income were designated exogenous. Even where agriculture is not the chief export activity, farm income has fluctuated so much that it is best considered independent of total personal income. Farm income varies widely with changes in weather, prices, and subsidies of federal crop support programs, all of which seem exogenous to an individual state. (In the personal income data, payments under these are included in farm income, not in transfer payments.)

All federal government salaries, both military and civilian, were assumed to be payments for exports of goods and services from the individual state to the nation as a whole. This assumption is patently true for defense payrolls, the biggest part of government salaries. Postal, judiciary, and similar functions are more nearly "local" and therefore more closely tied to total income. No adjustments were made to remove such items, because no clear criteria exist for exclusion of intermediate cases, and because extensive use of unpublished data would have been required for the period prior to 1958.

The "other industries" component of wages and salaries in personal incomes includes agricultural and similar service establishments, forestry, fisheries, and foreign government and international organization employment of United States residents (mostly in the metropolitan areas of New York and Washington, D.C.). Thus this component is best considered exogenous.

A Priori *Endogenous Income*

Some parts of personal income were considered endogenous because they depend upon developments of one sort or another within a state—though whether they depend specifically on income is open to question.

Three nonwage components treated as endogenous are "other labor income," nonfarm proprietors' income, and personal contributions to social insurance funds.

Most "other labor income" consists of employers' contributions to private pension and welfare funds (employers' contributions to *social* insurance funds are not part of personal income at all). Its volume is generally related to total wages and salaries, and in the official data state amounts are in fact estimated by state shares in certain payrolls. Much smaller amounts of "other labor income" represent military reserve inactive duty pay and compensation for employee injuries; the first should be exogenous, but since it is relatively small, separate information on its regional distribution is lacking. On the basis of employers' contributions, the entire component was included in Y_h.

Nonfarm proprietors were assumed to cater entirely to local demand. Industrial detail is lacking for their income, but the typical nature of their business is "local." Proprietors are chiefly in trades or professions and other services, all predominately local activities, and those in other industries are most likely to be owners of small firms which satisfy local demand.

The negative component of personal income, employee contributions for social insurance, is here part of Y_h. These payments are closely related to total wages and salaries, although rising tax rates and expanding coverage mean the relationship is not proportional. State amounts are officially estimated by state distributions of taxable payrolls. The component of course includes taxes withheld both on wages included in Y_h and in E. As leakages, part of them could be deducted directly from E rather than entirely from Y_h. While it may be preferable to handle them that way, since withheld taxes do not become part of even the "first round" of the multiplier process, it is unlikely that deducting them all from Y_h makes much difference in empirical results. (Simple national income models also deduct all withheld taxes from total income, even though some taxes apply to exogenous investment or government purchases and do not generate income even in the first round.)

As for wages and salaries, those in the following five industries are here considered endogenous, without regard to the location coefficient test:

(1) Construction: Although construction is investment, it is inherently *local,* and it was included in Y_h here because of its local character. In using the simple model, no attempt was made to disaggregate construction into parts which are dependent on total income, such as housing and construction of local industry plants, as against parts exogenously demanded, such as federal construction and construction of plants to produce for export markets. In a more involved treatment, it may be profitable to separate these two parts.

(2) State and local government: Here too, there are arguments for disaggregation. While state and local government employment undoubtedly depends on local growth and preferences, much of it may not depend on local income. Its independence is suggested by the fact that it has grown faster than total employment during the postwar period and has maintained its upward movement even during recessions. Yet, this growth may be considered merely a nonproportional *response* to total local income.

(3) Wholesale and retail trade: There is little question that retail trade depends upon total income. Wholesale trade may be open to question, but retail and wholesale trade combined is reported as a single figure in the personal income statistics. The covered wages data do show wholesale trade separately, but the coverage is not adequate because of the many small firms. Even so, the location coefficient test was applied to these covered wage figures; only for New York did the test clearly indicate that wholesale trade could be considered a significant export industry, and it was not included in E even for that state.

(4) Insurance agents and brokers, dealers in real estate, and combined real estate, law, and financial offices: These were assumed to cater chiefly to local demand. Insurance *carriers,* however, were included in the export sector in some states where the location coefficient criterion indicated they should be.

(5) Personal services and private households, business and repair services, professional, social, and related services: These were assumed to be responsive to local demand and dependent on total income. A few exceptions were made where other evidence was available. For example, SIC 73, Miscellaneous Business Services, was designated an export industry for New York because it includes advertising, and at one time included broadcasting. Medical service wages and salaries were included as significant export activities in Massachusetts and Minnesota, where concentrations of specialist hospitals are located; legal services in New York and Nevada, and nonprofit membership organizations in New York and Washington, D.C., were also designated export industries. All of these exceptions were supported by the location coefficient criterion as well as other evidence.

Coverage and Classification Changes
in the Covered Wages Data

Under the E_2 and E_3 definitions, export wages are made up in part of amounts reported by the Bureau of Employment Security (BES) in its quarterly bulletin, *Employment and Wages*.[1] These amounts are wages of workers covered by the state unemployment insurance programs. During the 1947-62 period, the reporting of these data was changed twice in ways which may affect the results of this study. These changes do not apply to the data used in estimating the E_1 definition of export wages.

In 1956, coverage of smaller firms was extended, and in 1958, a change was made in the industrial classification system used. In neither case can much be done to correct the possible distortions, nor is there sufficient evidence to quantify precisely the extent of the distortions. I feel, though, on the little evidence available, that the effects are not significant.

INCREASE IN COVERAGE. Before 1956 many states exempted from unemployment insurance tax, and thus from wage reporting, firms with less than eight employees. Beginning in 1956, no state could exempt firms with four or more employees. In addition, some states which already covered firms with four or more employees extended coverage to firms with even fewer than four. Altogether, thirty states were affected by these changes. Thus, beginning in 1956, some of the increases in the

---

[1] U. S. Bureau of Employment Security, *Employment and Wages of Workers Covered by State Unemployment Insurance Laws,* issued quarterly as a special issue of *Statistical Supplement to Labor Market and Employment Security.*

figures for E_2 and E_3 probably do not indicate growth in export activity since 1955 and earlier, but simply the inclusion of what were already export wages. This statement would be true if the small firms newly covered were in fact exporters. On the other hand, if they catered to local demand even in a predominately export industry, their inclusion would cause distortion because their wages would be mislabeled export wages. In either case, the growth in exogenous income is overstated and the growth in local income understated.

Information on the size distribution of firms in which covered wages are earned is available, but only starting with 1959, when the BES began to publish such data for the first quarter of each year (in each year's first quarterly issue of *Employment and Wages*). These 1959 data indirectly show the effect of the 1956 extension of coverage to smaller firms. The size-of-firm distribution is available by state, but only for industry groups much larger than two-digit industries. For national totals, however, size-of-firm data are given for all two-digit industries.

The effect of increased coverage must have varied from industry to industry, as the importance of small firms varies. In most states, the export industries for which BES data were used in this study are manufacturing industries. In manufacturing as a whole, the 1959 data show that small firms are relatively unimportant. The only size classes used by the 1959 data which would have been affected by the 1956 change are "less than 3 employees" and "4 to 9 employees." In the first quarter of 1959, of all the states which had made changes in 1956, only two (North Dakota and South Dakota) showed that more than 4 percent of their total manufacturing wages were earned in the size class which was affected by the state's change (the "4 to 9" size class in most states). Among the majority, in fact, less than 2 percent of total manufacturing wages was affected. This indication of the relatively low general importance of small firms suggests that extension of coverage to them had little distorting effect on the growth in export wages, and thus an even smaller effect on growth in total exogenous income. Even these low percentages are too high, in the sense that they include all employment in the "4 to 9" size class, whereas only firms with four to seven employees were affected by the 1956 changes. In neither of the two states where the percentage was greater than 4 percent is manufacturing a significant part of the export sector.

This is not entirely conclusive evidence. Manufacturing industries characterized by very small firms were much more significantly affected by the extension of coverage than were others. SIC industries 23 (Apparel), 24 (Lumber), 27 (Printing and Publishing), and 39 (Miscellaneous Manufacturing) are the important ones. In addition, small firms are important in some of the nonmanufacturing industries included in the export sector for some states and for which BES data were relied on. However, inspection of the composition of export wage income in each state reveals no case where such industries' wages make up so large a proportion of total exogenous income that growth rates would be significantly distorted by the 1956 change. Yet in the absence of more direct evidence, one cannot be absolutely sure of the magnitude of the distortion.

CHANGE IN INDUSTRIAL CLASSIFICATION. BES wage data were classified on the basis of the 1957 Standard Industrial Classification (SIC) effective in 1958. Previously the classification used was the 1945 SIC for manufacturing and the 1942 Social Security Board Industrial Classification Code for nonmanufacturing.

Not all industrial classification changes produced a distortion in the measurement of export wages under the E_2 and E_3 definitions. The size of a state's export sector is not changed by a transfer of production from one two-digit industry to another, if *both* are included in the export sector, or if *neither* is included. None of the analysis in this chapter or the next distinguishes between industries *within* the exogenous sector or *within* the local sector. What would cause distortion in the growth of exogenous income is a transfer of production between an export and a nonexport industry. This distortion would be significant to the extent the wages in the export industry are a relatively large part of exogenous income.

A special tabulation covering the first quarter of 1958 (in the first quarter 1958 issue of *Employment and Wages*) gives the only data on how the reclassification could have affected the results of this study. It compares the national totals for each industry's wages under the new classification with what they would have been under the old one. No data are given for separate states.

On the national level, the tabulation reveals the industries for which reclassification was significant. Significant reclassification can be judged to have occurred *either* when over 10 percent of the new industry's wages were earned in establishments not previously included in it, *or* when over 10 percent of the old industry's wages were earned in establishments not included in it in the new classification. The following describes the significant changes affecting industries included at any time in any state's export sector: SIC 19 (Ordnance) was enlarged at the expense of various unspecified industries; SIC 20 (Food Products) was enlarged by adding some activity previously classified as retail trade; SIC 30 (Rubber Products) was enlarged at the expense of SIC 39 (Miscellaneous Manufacturing); there was a good deal of reclassification from one industry to another within a particular group of three—SIC 34 (Fabricated Metal Products), SIC 35 (Nonelectrical Machinery), and SIC 36 (Electrical Machinery and Supplies); SIC 44 (Water Transportation) was enlarged at the expense of SIC 45 (Miscellaneous Transportation); SIC 73 was significantly reduced by transferring activities to SIC 49 (Communications) and to SIC 89 (Miscellaneous Services).

Inspection of the export sector for each state does reveal a number of states where these changes in classification may have had some net effect on the size of exogenous income in 1958 and later as compared with the period before 1958. There is no way to measure this distortion, because the 1958 recession is the obvious cause of many large changes between 1957 and 1958. However, there seems to be no state in which the above-named industries are relatively so important that the classification changes themselves produced a significant distortion. One cannot be certain about all this, but I feel that no major conclusion of this study is in danger on this score. The effects of these two breaks in continuity discussed here seem very small, at any rate, when compared with the difficulties in the general method itself of estimating export income.

CHAPTER IV

Testing the Model

$$(7) \qquad Y_h = \frac{a}{1-h} + \frac{h}{1-h} A$$

was fitted by least squares regression to the 1947-62 (annual) data for each state and region, using per capita variables. Three different definitions of A, exogenous income, were used for each state and region, as described in the previous chapter.

Table 7 summarizes the regression results. It shows the parameter estimates of a and h, as derived from the least-squares estimates of $a/(1-h)$ and $h/(1-h)$,[1] and the simple correlation coefficients for each of the three models tested.

The primary conclusion is that in general all three definitions of exogenous income produced very good fits, and that there is little basis for choosing one variant over another. For almost all states and regions, the three values of r, the correlation coefficient, are closely alike. Use of the significance test based on Fisher's z-transformation of r reveals that for only one state (Alaska) are two r's significantly different at the 5 percent level; there, the r for A_1 is

---

[1] Trygve Haavelmo, "Methods of Measuring the Marginal Propensity to Consume," *Journal of the American Statistical Association,* Vol. 42 (March 1947), pp. 108-09.

significantly different from the r for A_2, but not from the r for A_3.[2]

Except in the very few cases noted in the table, the estimates of h are highly significant, often ten to twenty times greater than their standard errors. It is true, however, that because of the pronounced trend in both independent and dependent variables, these are not spectacular results; the Durbin-Watson test indeed often shows significant autocorrelation (positive) in the residuals from the equation.[3] This means that the standard errors are frequently underestimated. The general relationship, however, is obviously significant. High correlations cannot be dismissed merely because the variables are time series with trends; such a situation merely requires that results be interpreted carefully. In the present case, it is the very relationship between the two trends which is of interest, since that relationship is the central specification of the model described.

Within each state and region, differences of closeness of fit are not statistically significant. It is of some interest, however, to note the ranking of the correlation coefficients. Of the sixty states and regions, the r for A_1 is highest in thirty-seven cases and second highest in fourteen; the r for A_2 is the highest in fourteen and second in twenty-nine; and the r for A_3 is highest in nine and second in seventeen. Moreover, there is an interesting regional variation in these rankings. In the seven New England cases (six states plus the region as a whole), the A_3 variant is highest five times; in the six East North Central cases, A_2 is highest in four.

Since the three models do not produce significantly different results in this regard, for the sake of economy in presentation, later estimates of the impact of defense spending in this work make use of two out of the three alternative figures for exogenous income, namely the A_1 and A_3 definitions. For many, but not all, of the later results, the figure for A_2 would be between the others in value, since for most states A_2 is between A_1 and A_3. It might

[2] See Maurice G. Kendall and Alan Stuart, *The Advanced Theory of Statistics,* Vol. 1 (London: Griffin, 1958), pp. 390-91, for the test appropriate for samples as small as the one here.

[3] According to the test, for each of the three models tested, about 40 percent of the sixty states and regions show definitely significant autocorrelation of residuals, about 35 percent are definitely not significant, and about 25 percent are inconclusive.

be added that the lack of significant differences may give some support to the use of A_3, the smallest estimate of exogenous income, since it seems plausible to explain the trend in endogenous income, and thus in total personal income, with a relatively small part of total personal income.

The use of per capita rather than alternative variables has probably reduced the closeness of fit. In a previous version of this study, only the A_2 definition of exogenous income was used, but both total and per capita forms of the variables were fitted for the 1947-61 period. The total variable form generally fitted slightly better than did the per capita variable, probably because the division of both dependent and independent variables by population removed some of the common trend.

Estimates of h and a

Table 7 shows that the estimates of h are highest, normally, for the A_3 variant, next highest for A_2 and lowest for A_1. There appears to be little systematic pattern in the signs and values of the estimates of a, except that the overwhelming majority of them are negative. This reflects the fact that, under any of the three definitions, endogenous or local income is growing faster than exogenous income, and that the ratio of local to total income is rising as the total is rising over time.

Regional base theory usually specifies, *ceteris paribus,* that the size of the "export" multiplier varies with the size of region under consideration. Large regions, that is, lose less than smaller ones through import leakage, since the larger the market the more easily it accommodates the minimum efficient sizes of more industries. *Ceteris paribus* is difficult to assume, however, because the value of h depends on induced investment as well as on import leakage, and induced investment may vary from region to region as a percentage of personal income. In the present context, differences in the size of h should show up most clearly in the results for the A_3 definition of exogenous income, because the other two definitions contain large amounts more correctly classified as local. Table 7 does show clearly higher estimates of h for several regions than for single states within a region, especially for the four regions west of the Mississippi and the South Atlantic Region. The results for the other regions are not convincing. The table also shows that some small states—small in the sense of size of the market—have unusually low estimates of h; these are the two Dakotas, Delaware, the District of Columbia, and Montana. But there are other small states, such as Vermont, many of the Mountain states, Alaska, and Hawaii, with normal or even higher estimates.

Cyclical Behavior

The local sector in each state contains many primarily local consumption goods industries and state and local government, the wages of which fall less than export wages and salaries or actually rise during recessions. Moreover, since the total exogenous part of income contains transfer payments and property income, it does not decline in recession as much as exports alone.

In view of the known stabilizing forces in consumption and state and local government, two models incorporating a "ratchet effect" were also tested. They were of the form:

(12) $$\frac{Y_h}{Y_p} = h' + b\frac{Y_p}{Y_p{}^o}, \quad \text{and}$$

(13) $$\frac{Y_h}{Y_p} = h' + b\frac{Y_p}{Y_p{}^o} + cY_p.$$

Equation (12) resembles one used by Duesenberry in his study of consumption.[4] The term $Y_p/Y_p{}^o$ is the ratio of present personal income to the previous peak level of personal income. Equation (13) adds as a variable personal income itself, to allow for a trend in the dependent variable which might appear if, for example, expanding size of market allowed import substitution. This personal income variable in the last term of (13) is *total* personal income in the state, but all other variables in the two equations are per capita. These two equations were fitted only to the definition of local income corresponding to the A_3 definition of exogenous income.[5]

The factors emphasized by Duesenberry, which prevent consumption from fluctuating as much as disposable income, would

[4] James S. Duesenberry, *Income, Saving, and the Theory of Consumer Behavior* (Harvard, 1949), p. 90.

[5] Both equations were fitted directly by least squares. Use of a reduced form method like equation (7) is not feasible in this case, as a very complicated nonlinear equation is the result. Advantages of consistent estimation techniques are in any case doubtful here because of the small number of observations.

TABLE 7. Regression Results for Three Definitions of Exogenous Income

State or Region	Correlation Coefficient			Estimate of h			Estimate of a^0		
	A_1	A_2	A_3	A_1	A_2	A_3	A_1	A_2	A_3
Maine	.973	.971	.967	.45	.48	.49	− 53	− 14	20
New Hampshire	.986	.985	.989	.45	.51	.59	− 77	−104	−104
Vermont	.967	.933	.954	.53	.63	.66	−153	−230	−144
Massachusetts	.990	.994	.995	.47	.49	.60	− 51	6	19
Connecticut	.976	.976	.982	.46	.51	.62	−120	−118	− 97
Rhode Island	.961	.948	.973	.48	.56	.63	−184	−207	−169
New England	.987	.990	.993	.47	.52	.62	− 85	− 43	− 33
New York	.994	.977	.995	.55	.46	.62	− 39	87	40
New Jersey	.987	.995	.994	.50	.59	.69	− 89	− 28	− 22
Pennsylvania	.994	.986	.989	.45	.57	.63	− 44	−124	9
Middle Atlantic	.994	.995	.992	.51	.47	.63	− 54	114	79
Ohio	.987	.988	.981	.46	.51	.63	− 63	− 1	− 15
Indiana	.964	.967	.962	.45	.50	.62	− 69	− 18	− 22
Illinois	.985	.988	.978	.52	.53	.67	−100	− 78	− 31
Michigan	.963	.960	.965	.47	.55	.63	−107	− 97	− 81
Wisconsin	.976	.973	.958	.47	.52	.62	− 91	− 43	− 39
East North Central	.982	.983	.976	.48	.54	.65	− 90	− 15	− 21
Minnesota	.972	.969	.958	.56	.63	.68	−101	−143	−128
Iowa	.856	.766	.717	.49	.55	.57	−105	−109	− 80
Missouri	.990	.981	.974	.50	.58	.64	− 34	− 49	− 18
North Dakota	.251	.249	.237	.18[a]	.19[a]	.18[a]	412	389	418
South Dakota	.568	.578	.518	.37[b]	.40[b]	.37[b]	93	55	136
Nebraska	.853	.815	.825	.50	.53	.55	− 46	−102	− 70
Kansas	.918	.898	.855	.49	.52	.55	− 45	− 96	− 50
West North Central	.955	.917	.903	.53	.63	.65	−106	−153	−122
Delaware	.987	.950	.945	.36	.38	.44	39	151	149
Maryland	.987	.994	.994	.47	.53	.56	− 5	99	113
District of Columbia	.972	.906	.920	.30	.17	.18	197	410	417

48

Virginia	.971	.947	.962	.48	.57	.59	− 81	− 155	− 88
West Virginia	.978	.948	.978	.53	.54	.57	− 151	− 156	− 99
North Carolina	.991	.988	.985	.49	.57	.62	− 99	− 131	− 147
South Carolina	.969	.973	.969	.45	.52	.57	− 67	− 106	− 106
Georgia	.984	.975	.977	.49	.59	.62	− 44	− 101	− 62
Florida	.982	.984	.983	.51	.57	.59	44	0	− 10
South Atlantic	.991	.989	.989	.50	.59	.61	− 76	− 100	− 63
Kentucky	.981	.953	.942	.46	.67	.67	− 51	− 148	− 116
Tennessee	.995	.990	.983	.50	.63	.67	− 50	− 86	− 63
Alabama	.983	.973	.963	.48	.56	.62	− 52	− 87	− 66
Mississippi	.949	.917	.919	.50	.60	.63	− 66	− 105	− 104
East South Central	.988	.978	.968	.49	.64	.67	− 57	− 126	− 80
Arkansas	.981	.969	.963	.46	.57	.60	− 44	− 124	− 106
Oklahoma	.980	.968	.963	.52	.59	.60	− 79	− 91	− 85
Louisiana	.985	.987	.981	.58	.60	.65	− 95	− 97	− 96
Texas	.988	.981	.974	.53	.60	.65	− 48	− 92	− 101
West South Central	.994	.989	.984	.54	.63	.66	− 70	− 127	− 121
Montana	.691	.664	.652	.48	.49	.50	− 23	− 94	− 18
Idaho	.941	.913	.902	.56	.59	.63	− 132	− 198	− 198
Wyoming	.777	.686	.705	.56	.55	.54	− 124	− 195	− 111
Colorado	.974	.975	.970	.60	.63	.66	− 165	− 95	− 112
Utah	.971	.955	.953	.49	.58	.60	3	− 90	− 40
Nevada	.619	.890	.896	.72[b]	.64	.65	− 216	− 318	− 275
Arizona	.853	.800	.798	.54	.60	.64	− 64	− 130	− 133
New Mexico	.919	.874	.876	.63	.62	.65	− 178	− 172	− 156
Mountain	.960	.937	.944	.61	.67	.68	− 185	− 255	− 201
Washington	.988	.984	.980	.47	.52	.56	13	0	17
Oregon	.985	.982	.973	.53	.59	.61	37	− 75	− 37
California	.975	.986	.982	.46	.55	.62	91	40	− 6
Pacific	.980	.976	.975	.47	.61	.62	79	− 15	− 44
Hawaii	.917	.882	.860	.55	.56	.60	− 267	− 256	− 267
Alaska	.142	.758	.611	.45[b]	.66	.75	− 57	− 744	57

Source: Calculated from data of the Office of Business Economics and the Bureau of Employment Security.

a Not statistically significant at the 5 percent level.

b Not statistically significant at the 1 percent level, but significant at the 5 percent level.

c No standard errors were computed for the estimates of α.

also help to make the parameter b negative. But b is also affected by induced investment, which would lead one to expect a positive effect, *a priori*, because rapid growth in personal income shows up as a higher ratio in relation to previous peak, and also induces more local investment than would a lower rate of growth. Use of a single aggregate for local income thus tends to hide some opposing tendencies and to reveal only a net result.

The use of equation (12) generally produced very poor fits to the data. The coefficients of correlation were extremely low and the estimate of b was statistically significant (at the 5 percent level) for only six states—Wisconsin, South Dakota, Kansas, Texas, Montana, and Wyoming—all of which characteristically experience great fluctuations in exogenous income. In about three-fourths of the sixty fits, the estimate of b was negative, as was to be expected from consideration of consumption theory alone.

Equation (13) produced much better fits to the data. Most of them are significant in a statistical sense, but in only eleven cases were the correlation coefficients higher than those which resulted from the fits of equation (7) using the A_3 variant.[6] These eleven cases are discussed in detail below.

In equation (13), the estimates of b were significant slightly more often than in equation (12). The summary of sign and significance (at the 5 percent level) of the estimates of b is as follows:

Sign	Cases in Which Significant	Cases in Which Not Significant	Total
+	1	11	12
−	17	31	48
Total	18	42	60

The estimates of c in equation (13) are often positive and statistically significant, as shown by this summary:

Sign	Cases in Which Significant	Cases in Which Not Significant	Total
+	40	11	51
−	5	4	9
Total	45	15	60

[6] This was true even when the r's for equation (7) and for equation (13) were both corrected for degrees of freedom. See H. Theil, *Economic Forecasts and Policy*, 2nd ed. (North-Holland, 1961), p. 212.

There were seventeen states or regions for which both the estimates of b and c in equation (13) were significant; in all but one case (Alaska), b was negative and c positive.[7]

The set of states for which c is negative is very similar to the set for which the estimate of a is positive in equation (7). This is the small set of states or regions for which the trend in the value of Y_h/Y_p was *downward* in the period. In the great majority the trend was upward, perhaps reflecting a lowering of import requirements as a result of one or both of the following factors: Markets may have expanded sufficiently to accommodate the minimum efficient sizes for certain industries; or consumption in general may have shifted toward services and away from durable goods, and thus increased the demand for local products at the expense of the kind often imported.

The eleven states for which equation (13) produced a better fit than equation (7) demonstrate the conditions under which the "ratchet" mechanism is most important. Table 8 lists these states, together with the parameter estimates and correlation coefficients from the fit of equation (13). Most of these states experienced large fluctuations in farm income. In the case of Iowa, for example, the estimates predict that a 10 percent drop in personal income below its previous peak will have the partial effect of raising the ratio of local to total income by 2.5 percentage points, and that a rise in personal income of $250 million will have the partial effect of raising the ratio by 1.0 percentage point. The two independent variables in equation (13) of course show opposing forces set up by any given movement in personal income relative to its previous peak, but the second term contributes to change only slowly over the long run.

A few final comments are in order. Over the postwar period, the *property income* part of exogenous income grew faster in most states than *export wage income*; that is, within variable A, variable P grew somewhat faster than variable E. This holds for all three alternative definitions of E discussed in this work. It is also interesting to note the results of fitting the following equation, which was done in

---

[7] Unfortunately, the residuals from equation (13) are also plagued by positive autocorrelation. The Durbin-Watson test shows about 40 percent definitely significantly autocorrelated, about 25 percent definitely not, and about 35 percent where the test is inconclusive.

TABLE 8. Estimates in the Ratchet Form of the Model

State	Estimates of Parameters			Correlation Coefficient[b]
	h'	b	$100c^a$	
Iowa	.62	−.25	.004	.880
North Dakota	.58	− 46	.038	.841
South Dakota	.66	−.41	.020	.848
District of Columbia	.55	+.01[c]	−.010	.949
Montana	.74	−.35	.009	.931
Idaho	.57	−.18	.012	.956
Wyoming	.64	−.25	.014	.831
Nevada	.62	−.15	.012	.913
Arizona	.56	−.08	.004	.867
Hawaii	.37	−.02	.011	.917
Alaska	.05	+.21	.033	.953

Source: Calculated from data of the Office of Business Economics and the Bureau of Employment Security.
[a] The estimate of c has been multiplied by 100 for easier comprehension.
[b] Correlation coefficients are unadjusted for degrees of freedom.
[c] All parameter estimates except this one are significant at the 5 percent level.

the earlier version of this study for the 1947-61 period, using the A_2 definition of exogenous income:

$$(14) \qquad Y_h = a' + b'P + c'E.$$

Both the partial correlation coefficients and the tests of significance on the regression coefficients showed that the explanatory power of P alone was considerably greater than that of E alone. (The estimate of a' was also more often positive than the estimate of a in equation (7).) The poor explanatory power of E stems mostly from the fact that it typically declines greatly in recession, while P does not; this highly stabilizing effect of P provides a floor for Y_h, thus P and Y_h are more closely related than E and Y_h.

The conclusion to be drawn from all these results is that the simple model explains movements in local incomes, and thus in total personal income, rather well. The ratio of local income to total income is not constant, but there is a strong linear correlation between exogenous income, variously defined, and local income. The cases where this is not true were in states which experienced severe fluctuations in exogenous income; for these states a different model is suitable, but it also allows one to place major emphasis on the exogenous sector as the main long-term influence on total income.

For all states, therefore, the relationship between defense-derived income and total exogenous income seems a subject worthy of extended analysis. Since the tests have demonstrated the usefulness of one of the three measures of exogenous income as the major explanatory variable, the role of defense income as a part of exogenous income can be justified as the focus of further inquiry into the impact of defense spending on regional growth.

CHAPTER V

Estimation of Defense Purchases by State

THE DEFENSE EXPENDITURES analyzed in this study are the *purchases of goods and services* in the United States by the Department of Defense, under the federal budget's functional titles "Military Functions," and "Foreign Military Assistance." The Department of Defense includes the three military services or departments—Army, Navy, and Air Force—and unified procurement agencies such as the Defense Supply Agency. Nonpurchase expenditures are not considered.[1]

The amounts by state of military and civilian wages and salaries are taken directly from personal income data of the Office of Business Economics, some of which are unpublished. These data are briefly described in the appendix to this chapter. The rest of the chapter describes the procedures used to estimate procurement.

---

[1] The nonpurchase expenditures are retirement pay and certain outright grants. Also excluded are expenditures by other agencies under the broader Major National Security title for stockpiling, atomic energy development (including nuclear warheads), and miscellaneous items. These are excluded because data on their regional distribution are unavailable.

Estimates of Procurement

Only estimates of uncertain reliability can be made of annual procurement purchases by state. Since even these estimates involve complex conceptual and practical questions, it is not surprising that previous regional studies of defense purchases have found procurement most difficult to treat, and that a variety of approaches and techniques for its estimation have resulted.

Data on procurement *purchases* are available only as national totals, not differentiated by region. Data are available on *prime contracts* by state, and they are described in detail in the appendix to this chapter. For the moment, it seems useful to note only that contract value is classified by state and by "procurement program" ("aircraft," "missiles," and so forth), but that since these classifications are not simultaneous except for a very few recent years, the composition of contracts in each state is not known for most of the period of heavy expenditures.

The two main difficulties in the use of the prime contract statistics, as noted earlier, are that purchases are spread out over some years after a contract is granted, and subcontracting and other purchasing by prime contractors results in much value added being produced outside the state where the contract is let. Every serious study of the regional distribution of defense purchases has recognized these two problems, whether the prime contract data were presented with or without adjustment. A third problem is that the official statistics usually classify the entire value of a contract in the state where most of the work is to be done. In practice, since many large contractors have a number of plants in several different states, even the final assembly work is sometimes done in more than one state. This factor causes the same distortion as that resulting from subcontracting.

The distribution of contracts by state is of some interest, for it indicates location of later stages of production—final fabrication and assembly. But the share of value added in earlier stages is high and represents a sizeable demand in many other states. From specific sample studies and general interindustry and interregional trading patterns, it is known that many different states produce parts of value added in a large military order or a large group of small orders.[2]

Estimates of procurement were made here by estimating annual percentage *shares* for each state, and then multiplying them by the national purchases total.[3] These shares are prime contract shares adjusted for the lag of purchases in time and for the dispersion of value added by contractors' out-of-state purchases. The adjustments of contract shares are similar in outline to some used in previous studies, but they differ in detail. Table 9 summarizes the methods of the most important earlier studies, along with the adjustments used here. It can be seen that previous studies have either concentrated upon a few years or a few states.

Some of the authors of these earlier studies made no timing adjustments, for they assumed that the amount of purchases is equal to contract value for a given year, and that contract shares need be adjusted only for the geographical dispersion of value added. It seems preferable to use a moving average of contract shares in the current and the two previous calendar years. A large part of purchases is made only after the year of the contract, but almost all the contract is usually paid for within three years. Algebraically, this is expressed:

$$(15) \qquad s_{it} = p_1\ c_{it} + p_2\ c_{it-1} + p_3\ c_{it-2}$$
$$(p_1 + p_2 + p_3 = 1),$$

where i and t are subscripts denoting state and year, respectively; s is the share of purchases, adjusted for timing but not for dispersion of value added; c is the share of total prime contract value in the nation; and p_1 is the percentage of contract value paid for within one year; p_2, the percentage in the second year after placement; p_3, the percentage in the third year. Later in the chapter, the specific values used for p_1, p_2, and p_3 are explained in the light of evidence.

[2] To date, the few sample studies available are not representative or detailed enough to allow one to infer the actual geographic pattern of value added. Some of these studies are reported by United Aircraft Company for 1955 in *The Aircraft Industry,* Hearing before the House Select Committee on Small Business, 84 Cong. 2 sess. (1956), p. 241.

[3] All purchase value is assumed to be produced in the United States; the value of materials and services imported from abroad by contractors is not eliminated. Purchases abroad by the military services, however, are excluded.

As for dispersion adjustments, all the studies cited in Table 9 gave only partial weight to prime contract shares (after timing adjustment, if any), and gave some weight to states' shares in other distribution, notably wages or value added in certain industries. The general scheme is:

$$(16) \qquad v_{it} = \alpha s_{it} + \beta x_{1t} + \gamma x_{2t} + \delta x_{3t} + \ldots,$$

where i and t denote state and year, respectively; v is the estimated share of purchases; s is the prime contract shares adjusted for timing, as determined by equation (15); and x_1, x_2, x_3 . . . are shares in other relevant distributions, weighted by β, γ, δ, . . . , respectively.

Any number of x variables can be used, so long as the weights add up to $(1 - \alpha)$. The rationale for using any particular distribution is that state shares in it offer "clues" on the distribution of value added in defense production. It should be noted that the x variables are for the same period as the estimate of value added. If, instead, they were moving averages like the s variable, a different rationale would be implied—the x distributions would be treated as *determinants* of the dispersion of subcontracts and other purchases by prime contractors. This alternative could be justified if the distributions were of *capacity* and if it were assumed that dispersion reflects capacity. The actual procedure uses x variables which are indicators of *output,* with an implicit assumption that defense production (within the industries making up one x variable) was geographically distributed in the same way as total output.

One previous study is not described in Table 9 because it did not use prime contract data. For fiscal year 1952, Selma Mushkin used input-output analysis to estimate the incidence of defense purchases by state.[4] She assumed the 1952 bill of goods was similar to that for 1944, on which information was available. Using a 1939 input-output table, she derived the direct and indirect requirements broken down by industry. Total purchases were distributed according to states' shares in wages in the various industries, each of which was weighted by the total shipments (for direct and indirect demand) from it.

---

[4] Selma J. Mushkin, *Statistical Materials on the Distribution of Federal Expenditures Among the States* (U. S. Public Health Service, 1956); Selma J. Mushkin, "Distribution of Federal Expenditures Among the States," *Review of Economics and Statistics,* Vol. 39 (November 1957), pp. 435-50.

TABLE 9. Summary of Procurement Estimation Methods

Author and Scope	National Purchases Total Used	Timing			Dispersion, Distributions, and Weights		
		P_1	P_2	P_3	α	Defense-Related Industries	Other Distributions
Labovitz[a]							
All States							
Fiscal Year 1958							
Major Hard Goods	Prime contract totals	1	0	0	.4[d]	Value added in SIC 36, 37, 38, 19 .1	Value added in all manufacturing .2
						Value added in same excluding 371, 374 .3	
Other Goods	Prime contract totals	1	0	0	0	None	Military payrolls 1
Construction	Prime contract totals	1	0	0	1	None	None
Upper Midwest Economic Study[b]							
All States, Fiscal Years 1952 and 1960							
Construction	Prime contract totals	1	0	0	1	None	None
Under $10,000	Prime contract totals	1	0	0	0	None	Military payrolls 1

58

	Method					Value added / Wages detail	All other manufacturing
All Other	Prime contract totals	1	0	0	.5	Not detailed, but Labovitz cited. Weight of .5	
Pfister[a] New England States, Fiscal Years 1954 and 1958	Moving average of prime contract totals, with same weights as the p's	.4	.4	.2	.4	Value added in SIC 372, 373, 366, 367, 381, 19. Weight of .32 Value added in SIC 291, 33, 35, 36. Weight of .08	Value added in all manufacturing .2
Present Study All States for All Years 1951–62	Defense purchases series of national accounts	.6	.3	.1	.5	Wages in SIC 372, 373, 366, 367, 381, 19. Alternative weights of .3 .2, and .1[e]	Wages in all other manufacturing. Alternative weights of .2, .3, and .4

---

[a] U. S. Library of Congress, Federal Taxation and Expenditures in the Several States (1959), by I. M. Labovitz. The procurement estimates presented there are part of estimates of all federal taxes and expenditures by state for fiscal year 1958.

[b] Upper Midwest Economic Study, The Geographic Impact of the Federal Budget (1962). (No author specified, but preface gives major credit to John Adams and Ronald J. Wonnacott.)

[c] Richard L. Pfister, Military Expenditures in New England (Federal Reserve Bank of Boston, 1961), pp. 3–4. The details of the estimates are a little different for 1954. Pfister's avowed goal was not to estimate the distribution of value added at all stages, but only to allocate to each state value added to components purchased by final-assembly plants in addition to value added in final assembly itself. Pfister also made alternative estimates in a way which did not use the data on prime contracts by state at all. He distributed total contract value in various procurement programs according to states' shares in employment in roughly comparable SIC industries.

[d] The total of Major Hard Goods contracts in this study was distributed by giving a weight of .4 to the distribution of contracts for all programs.

[e] For years 1951–53, some weight was also given to SIC industries 371 and 354. See later discussion in this chapter.

This seems the most satisfactory conceptual method, if used in conjunction with the prime contract data. But no up-to-date input-output table was available when this was written; since the date the most recent table was issued, inter-industry relations in defense production changed substantially. Moreover, much work would have been required to estimate accurately the bill of goods for each year, since that had also changed greatly. A shortcoming of this conceptual method is that input-output coefficients are for shipments, not value added, and the weights therefore may not be appropriate; they would be identical to weights for value added only if all industries have the same ratio of value added to value of shipments.

The rest of this chapter describes the evidence which favors the specific adjustments made in this study.

The Timing Adjustments

The timing adjustments apply only to estimation of state *shares*. For national totals, the Office of Business Economics annual series of purchases was used. As is pointed out in the appendix to this chapter, that series presents difficulties for short-run analysis, since its timing is not the same as that of actual production. For a long-run analysis which concentrates on changes between representative years, the difficulties are not serious. The explanation in the appendix to this chapter is included primarily as a warning to any reader who might plan to use the annual estimates presented in the General Appendix for study of short-run changes.

The use of .6, .3, and .1 for p_1, p_2, and p_3, respectively, is based on information on the timing of budget expenditures after legislative appropriations, and on the pattern of obligation (roughly coincident with contracting) after appropriation.[5] The two patterns give a rough indication of the lag of expenditures after contracts.[6]

For most procurement programs in recent years the great bulk of expenditures have been made within three years of appropria-

---

[5] This information was provided by various parts of the Office of the Secretary of Defense. I am especially indebted to Phil O'Deen for aid in its collection.

[6] For some projects with a security classification, the timing estimates used arbitrarily assume all the appropriation will be spent within one year, a possible source of bias.

tion. The amounts not expended until the fourth and later years are usually less than 10 percent of total cost. Since some *obligations* do not fall until the second or third year of "project life," the expenditures made later than three years after the *contract* date are not significant. For example, about 10 percent of expenditures for Air Force non-ballistic missiles is not made until the fourth and fifth years; on the other hand, 15 percent is not obligated until the second year and 5 percent not until the third.

A part of shipbuilding is the only important exception to the three year rule of thumb. The rule holds for ship conversion and construction of Polaris submarines. For other new construction, just over half of all expenditures is estimated to come after the third year, with 6 per cent made as late as the sixth and seventh years after appropriation. About 90 percent of obligations are incurred within the three years (60 percent in the first year), so a significant portion of expenditures obviously comes more than three years after the contract date.

The time pattern *within* the first three years varies. The average lag for research and development expenditures after contract is probably less than a year, and not much more for construction. For ballistic missiles the lag is surprisingly short; almost all expenditures probably are made within two years of obligation. For aircraft, non-ballistic missiles, and army procurement generally, the average lag appears to be somewhat longer, with large expenditures being made in the third year after contract. The lag appears to be less than two years for ship conversion; for new construction other than of Polaris submarines, as noted above, it is much longer. The lag for Polaris falls between the lags for ship conversion and for other new construction.

The above patterns do not apply to routine purchases of "off-the-shelf" operating supplies and equipment. These comprise a large part of total volume, and the lag in expenditure for them is extremely short; orders are often filled out of inventory by suppliers. (Although there are term contracts for frequently purchased items, amounts are not included in the prime contract series until actual job orders, purchase orders, or delivery orders are issued.) After allowance was made for this and for the patterns for items with longer lead times, the values of .6, .3, and .1 for p_1, p_2, and p_3

were decided upon; no allowance was made for the very long lag for some shipbuilding because it applies to a relatively small part of procurement.

These time patterns were applied to all states. Since actual time lags vary from program to program, the correct patterns also vary with the composition of each state's contracts. No allowance could be made for this fact, however, because no simultaneous classification by state and by program exists for the period before fiscal year 1961.

The time patterns were also applied to all years of the 1951-62 period,[7] even though the average lag may have shortened recently as a result of relative increases in research and development, the lack of large swings in volume, and the emergence of excess capacity in the airframe industry. Lack of data and my desire for a computationally simple procedure required a uniform pattern.[8]

Reasons other than the importance of "off-the-shelf" purchases account for the large proportion of contract value paid for within one year. Periodic cost-reimbursement or progress payment arrangements are common; expenditures thus start before delivery and perhaps soon after the contract is let. Some companies expect a fairly steady stream of contracts, and thus maintain a certain minimum capacity which allows them to respond to contracts quickly. Such companies have specialized skills, or by winning contracts in

[7] Since contracts by state are reported only after the middle of 1950, the 1951 values of s_{it} were calculated by weighting the 1951 contract shares by 60 percent and the shares for the second six months of 1950 by 40 percent. The 1952 values of s_{it} use the second six-month period of 1950 for year t-2. Percentage shares for Alaska and Hawaii are available only from 1956 on; for these, the s_{1956} is equal to c_{1956}, and s_{1957} is equal to .6 c_{1957} plus .4 c_{1956}.

[8] Attempts to estimate a distributed lag by regression did not prove profitable. Fitting national purchases in year t to the national contracts in years t, t-1, and t-2 gave the following equation when a fit was forced through the origin:

Purchases$_t$ = .73 C_t − .04 C_{t-1} + .37 C_{t-2}.

The period covered was 1953-60. Neither the negative coefficient for C_{t-1} nor the large one for C_{t-2} is acceptable in the light of independent evidence. The multiple correlation coefficient (R) for this fit was .60. When a constant was allowed, the result was:

Purchases$_t$ = 12.7 + .23 C_t + .16 C_{t-1} + .11 C_{t-2}.

The constant is in billions; it accounts for about half of purchases in many years. The multiple correlation coefficient was .86. But, of course, forcing the equation through the origin is more reasonable, considering the economic meaning of the equation.

the past are almost certain to receive natural "follow-on" contracts later (a company producing planes is likely to get the contract for their spare parts; a missile manufacturer will probably be hired to test and install his product, and so forth). A firm may depend on its research to lead to development and production contracts, and thus maintain capacity and personnel—especially scientific personnel for whom demand is great—to fulfill later orders with only a short delay. Such firms may be perfectly confident of winning a contract long before negotiations are formally completed and before the award is recorded in the contract series.

Some contracts are really made after the fact and are legal formalities to cover completed work. Others may cover extra costs incurred, either because of inaccurate original estimates or changed specifications. Credit changes may reflect cost savings. Such changes are important because of the uncertainties and exploratory nature of defense production. In these cases, the timing in the contract statistics actually lags behind the economic impact.

Finally, many research and development contracts are granted on a "level of effort" basis, which covers costs—of man hours, for example—necessary to maintain a certain volume of work on a given problem; these costs are reimbursed periodically.[9]

The Dispersion Adjustments

The weighted average of distributions used in this study can be expressed as follows, in order to establish notation used hereafter:

$$(17) \qquad v_{it} = \alpha s_{it} + \beta d_{it} + (1 - \alpha - \beta) m_{it},$$

where i and t denote state and year, respectively; v is the estimated share of purchases; s is the contract share, adjusted for timing, as determined by equation (15); d is the share in wages in "defense-related" industries; and m is the share in wages in all other manufacturing industries.

The dependence on contracts is obvious, for a large fraction of value is added by the prime contractor. Even some earlier-stage defense production is specialized, so the distribution of certain "defense-related" industries, such as aircraft and ordnance, should be

[9] Statement by Charles J. Hitch in *Inventory Fluctuations and Economic Stabilization*, Hearing before the Joint Economic Committee, 87 Cong. 2 sess. (1962), p. 115.

considered. In the end, all defense items contain ordinary parts and materials, so more general manufacturing is also relevant. "General" or "other" manufacturing here means all manufacturing except specified defense-related industries.

Some purchases by contractors are of nonmanufactured services. These tend to be located in the same state as the manufacturing they serve, and the distribution of value added in them is assumed to be like that of manufacturing value added. If the military services buy such services directly, the prime contracts themselves reflect it.

Value added data are not available for many defense-related industries for all states, due to severely restrictive disclosure rules in the Census of Manufactures. Data on wages by industry and state are used here as an approximation of the distribution of output.[10]

Each weight, α, β, and $(1 - \alpha - \beta)$, has distinct meaning. That of prime contracts, α, should be the average proportion of contract value added in the prime contractor's own establishment—the fraction assumed to "stay" inside his own walls. The value of β is the proportion produced outside prime contractors' plants but in the defense-related industries, either in the prime contractor's state or outside it. The value of $(1 - \alpha - \beta)$ is the proportion produced in other manufacturing industries, within or outside of the contractor's state. The second and third terms of (17) assign to a state all value

[10] The following wages data were used: Defense-related industries: U. S. Bureau of Employment Security data published in its *Employment and Wages of Workers Covered by State Unemployment Insurance Laws*, special issue of *Statistical Supplement to Labor Market and Employment Security* (quarterly issues, 1951-62). The few amounts not disclosed in these statistics were estimated on the basis of interpolation, regional totals, and totals for more aggregated industry groupings. The appendix to this chapter examines two reporting changes, one in 1956 and one in 1958, which cause breaks in continuity of these data and which may affect the regional distributions. The breaks are not serious enough to change any major conclusion of this study.

Total manufacturing: U. S. Office of Business Economics series in its *Personal Income by States since 1929*, a supplement to the *Survey of Current Business* (1956), and in articles (variously titled) on personal income by states in *Survey of Current Business*, Vols. 39-43 (August issues, 1959-63). While the Bureau of Employment Security figures are more than satisfactory for the specific defense-related industries, the Office of Business Economics figures for total manufacturing wages are used because they have slightly broader coverage than the Bureau of Employment Security figures for total manufacturing.

Other or general manufacturing: Total manufacturing minus defense-related, both from the sources just described.

sold by its subcontractors and other vendors, whether to prime contractors located in the same state or in other states.

Weight for Prime Contract Distribution

There is evidence for use of .5 as the value of α. The Department of Defense, in connection with a small business promotion program, has for some years collected information from large contractors on total payments to outside suppliers. Table 10 summarizes

TABLE 10. Outside Payments by Large Defense Contractors, 1957–62

(Dollar figures in millions)

	FY 1957	1958	1959	1960	1961	1962
Number of large contractors reporting	298	294	298	298	309	378
Receipts from both prime and subcontract work	$16,992	17,479	18,704	19,095	19,803	22,237
Subcontract and other outside payments	$9,314	9,026	9,144	9,666	9,407	10,560
Subcontract receipts as percent of total receipts	54.8	51.6	48.9	50.6	47.5	47.5

Source: U. S. Department of Defense, *Military Prime Contract Awards and Subcontract Payments* (July–December 1962), p. 44.

the reports. About 50 percent of the value of large prime contracts and subcontracts has been spent for outside purchases. This average conceals a great deal of variation from program to program and from firm to firm, of course.[11]

[11] Various percentages have been revealed in congressional hearings by contractors and the Defense Department. For examples, see the following: *The Aircraft Industry,* Hearing before the House Select Committee on Small Business, 84 Cong. 2 sess. (1956), pp. 44, 75, 78, 105, 145, 241, 259; *The Aircraft Industry,* Hearing before the House Select Committee on Small Business, 85 Cong. 2 sess. (1959), pp. 68, 90, 199 (ballistic missile contractors); *Small Business Participation in Defense Subcontracting,* Hearing before the Senate Select Committee on Small Business, 86 Cong. 1 sess. (1959), pp. 150, 156-57, 182, 214, 253, 256, 265; *Department of Defense Appropriations for 1963,* Hearing before the House Committee on Appropriations, 87 Cong. 2 sess. (1962), Pt. 4, pp. 163 (Navy aircraft), 309 (intercontinental ballistic missile contractors); *Military Procurement,* Hearing before the Senate Armed Services Committee (1959), p. 109.

Such a high fraction is not peculiar to defense production; large industries producing for civilian demand show similarly high fractions. What is peculiar is the heavy use of the subcontract as a particular legal instrument; in fact, it is common to use the term "subcontracting" to denote all purchases by prime contractors, whether in that legal form or not. It is not known if the ratio has increased or decreased over the period of heavy defense expenditures, except for the period covered by the surveys. The type of work subcontracted has definitely changed, just as has the composition of defense spending. In the days of long production runs in World War II and the Korean War, "overflow" subcontracting was common due to the limits on physical capacity. Later, when weapons systems became more complex and began to be produced in small lots, technical rather than physical capacity forced specialized subassemblies to be subcontracted to companies with skills the prime contractor did not have.

An increase in complexity would seem likely to increase the ratio, but shorter production runs, increasing emphasis on labor-intensive research and development, and excess capacity in the airframe industry all tend to counteract such an increase. (There has been extensive designation of "integrating" or "managing" prime contractors, with separate prime contracts being let for major components, but this use of "government-furnished equipment" was also common in World War II and the Korean War.)

For years prior to the surveys summarized in Table 10, a few samples support the use of .5 as the average subcontracting percentage.[12] In the airframe industry alone, however, the ratio fluctuated with the volume of orders—rising, for example, when military demand rose suddenly.[13] The use of .5 for the entire

[12] In 1953, 100 large Air Force prime contractors, holding contracts amounting to $15.5 billion, reported that 52 percent of the contract value had been committed for purchases from other firms. For fiscal year 1954, 35 major aircraft and parts manufacturers reported to the Aircraft Industries Association that 54 percent of all disbursement (excluding taxes but including outside purchases, payrolls, dividends, and reinvested earnings) was paid to subcontractors and other suppliers. These two results are reported in *The Aircraft Industry* (1956), pp. 102, 109, and 234. In 1953 the Army reported a 56 percent ratio for a sample of 13 contractors receiving $168 million in contracts, in *Military Procurement*, Hearing before the Senate Select Committee on Small Business, 83 Cong. 1 sess. (1953), p. 411.

[13] *The Aircraft Industry* (1956), p. 75.

1951-62 period, therefore, is based only on partial evidence for the first half of the period.

The value of α is based on data on purchases outside the *firm*. A higher weight for contracts may be thought desirable, because a contractor will spend more in his own state than is indicated by that state's shares in the other distributions. First, most of the local trade and service needs will be met in the same state; second, suppliers in the state may have an economic advantage in being near the contractor, due to lower transport costs or other benefits of proximity. (However, many purchases are of parts with high value per unit of weight; for these, transport costs are less important.) No correction is made for this variable, because certain defects in the contract statistics themselves seem to offset it. Some contracts are recorded in the state of the head office of the contractor, even if assembly takes place in another, and an entire amount is sometimes recorded in one state when assembly actually takes place in two different states. These errors tend to overstate the value for the state in which the contract is reported, somewhat offsetting the understatement referred to just above. They also tend to underestimate procurement in states where plants, but not head offices, are located.

Defense-Related Industries

An industry should be designated "defense-related" only if it is both important for defense production and one within which defense production is a large part of its total output. Only then does it make sense to separate the regional distribution of defense-related industries from other manufacturing industries. Two which most obviously qualify are SIC 372, Aircraft and Parts, and SIC 19, Ordnance. Over the entire period these industries produced primarily for defense demand. While guns, ammunition, bombs, and tanks were much less important after the Korean War, SIC 19 continues to qualify because it includes work on complete guided missiles (missile components and subsystems are classified in other industries).

As shown in Table 9, four other industries are here included for all the years 1951-61: SIC 366, Communications Equipment; SIC 367, Electronic Components and Accessories; SIC 373, Ships and Boats; and SIC 381, Engineering, Laboratory, and Scientific and

Research Instruments. (Prior to 1958, SIC 367 did not exist as a separate industry; most relevant establishments were classified in SIC 366.)

All six of these industries of course also produce for civilian markets. Since its geographical distribution of the civilian production may differ from that of defense production, use of the aggregate industry is a simplification. However, beginning with 1958, neither SIC 366 nor SIC 367 includes household appliances or domestic radio and television receivers, although home receivers were included in SIC 366 before 1958. SIC 381 excludes surgical, dental, photographic, and automatic temperature control instruments.

Obligations data for the Korean period indicate that two other industries should be added for 1951-53. The military bill of goods then included large amounts for motor vehicles and production equipment; over $7 billion was spent for such items in fiscal years 1951-53. Many vehicles were not for "combat," and even combat vehicles used parts produced in SIC 371, Motor Vehicles, rather than in SIC 19, Ordnance. As for production equipment, inspection of three-digit categories within SIC 35, Machinery, suggests that SIC 354, Metalworking Machinery, was the most suitable industry to include. SIC 371 and 354 were not included in their entirety, because they included so much civilian production; moreover, since they were eliminated from the defense-related group starting with 1954, their full inclusion in 1951-53 would cause unrealistic swings in the estimates. The appendix to this chapter explains the determination of fractions of SIC 371 and 354 included for 1951-53, and it supplies information on the relative importance of defense production among the other six included in the defense-related group.

Weight for Distribution of Defense-Related Wages

For some items of procurement, the distribution of defense-related industry should be given a weight of zero, since they are common, ordinary items used for general housekeeping and maintenance, and produced by general manufacturing firms. These "off-the-shelf" goods and services are produced mostly for civilian use, and they are not even fabricated to unusual specifications for the military.

At the other extreme, and quite a bit larger in total value, are weapons systems made only for defense use. In these the value of β should be high, although not as high as 1-α, since even the most specialized weapons require at some stage of production rather common materials and parts. Since the evidence for values of β is not as clear as for α, the estimates here were first made using three alternative values of β, .1, .2, and .3. On the basis of equation (16), it may be seen that:

$$v_{it} = \beta(d_{it} - m_{it}) + (1 - \alpha)m_{it} + \alpha s_{it}.$$

Given some t, there is a rather low correlation between d_{it} and m_{it}, especially in recent years, so variation in β does produce significant changes in v, especially for certain states with substantial differences between d and m. Even if absolute variation in v is not great, percentage variation can be.

Variability of Estimates

Estimates of v_{it}, and the corresponding dollar amounts of procurement purchases, for all twelve years of the period and for all states and census regions, are presented in the General Appendix, Table A-2; in each case estimates are shown for the alternative values of β.

The General Appendix table shows substantial movement in v, as β is varied, for some states and regions, but insignificant movement for others. Where there was a sizeable spread, it usually increased in the second half of the period, because the correlation between d and m declined. Among regions, spreads are widest for the Pacific and East North Central, which had great differences between shares of defense-related industries and other manufacturing. Some of the increased spread in the later 1950's was due to elimination of vehicles and production equipment from the defense-related group after the Korean War; for both the Pacific and East North Central Regions, for example, this change increased substantially the difference between d and m.

During the Korean period, the Pacific Region's spread was about 2 percentage points, or $0.5 billion; in 1962 it had reached over 4.5 points, or more than $1.3 billion. From a narrow spread during the Korean War, the range of estimates for the East North

Central Region rose in 1962 to nearly 4.0 points, or about $1 billion.

Variation was not large for the West North Central, West South Central, and Mountain Regions; in each case the spread was less than a percentage point all through the period. While fluctuating somewhat, the Middle Atlantic Region's range was above one point in only three of the eleven years, and that for the South Atlantic above half a point in only two.

Among individual states which are later shown to be important in defense procurement, the spreads are rather large for California, Michigan, and Pennsylvania. California's is very large, reaching four percentage points (about $1 billion) in 1962; for Michigan and Pennsylvania, spreads of a point or so are common. No other state has a spread of more than one percentage point for any year. The ranges are very narrow for the important states of New York, Missouri, Virginia, Georgia and Colorado, and only moderately wide for Texas, Florida and Arizona. This is itself a significant result, showing that many estimates are not extremely sensitive to variations in the weight given to the distribution of defense-related industries.

Appendix to Chapter V

Military Payrolls

FIGURES FOR MILITARY PAYROLLS, as published by the Office of Business Economics,[1] are estimates with considerable margin of error, but are used here with no modification.

Reserve forces' inactive duty pay is not included. It is instead part of another component of personal income called "other labor income," and the estimates of it by state are not published separately. The omission results in a very minor inconsistency since the *procurement* estimates of this study are meant to include Department of Defense purchases for reserve forces.

Based on the "personal income where received" concept, payrolls include pay in kind—that is, food and clothing furnished enlisted personnel. These items are not included in procurement purchases.[2] However, the estimates of procurement *shares* developed here are based on states' prime contract shares, and these shares are of procurement contract value including subsistence and clothing. This difference in the contract statistics and the purchases total for the nation thus leads to a small inconsistency. It is a difference between the content of the total to be allocated and of one of the series used to allocate it, not a difference in overall coverage, and there is no overstatement of the national total of purchases. Since this study's estimates of purchases by state were made with considerable unavoidable margin of error in the first place, the small improvement in accuracy which would result from elimination of the inconsistency seems unwarranted.

The official payroll figures properly exclude net pay to personnel overseas, and rightly transfer dependents' allotments from the state of duty station to the state of residence of dependents. Although these changes are estimated, and are therefore somewhat unreliable, they are necessary if the payroll figures are to be used for regional macroeconomic analysis. The net pay—gross pay minus dependents' allotments—of

[1] U. S. Office of Business Economics, *Personal Income by States since 1929,* a supplement to the *Survey of Current Business* (1956), pp. 95-97 and 100-01; and articles on personal income by states (variously titled), in *Survey of Current Business,* Vols. 39-43 (August issues, 1959-63).

[2] Not all subsistence and clothing purchased is included in the payrolls by state. Clothing which is not "standard issue" is excluded, and so are food and clothing purchased in the United States for use by personnel stationed abroad.

overseas personnel probably generates little demand in this country, although some expenditure here is made through channels other than allotments. Allotments are consumed or saved in the state where they are received, not the state of duty station, since they are deducted from the pay of personnel.

The official estimates are made by distributing the national total of net pay among states according to the distribution of military strength, with the allocations being made separately for officers and enlisted men, and by distributing the total allotments received by dependents in the United States according to the sum of the distributions of military strength and civilian population.

Civilian Wages and Salaries

The figures for these kinds of purchases are much more reliable than the ones for procurement or military pay. Except for 1947-48 and 1954, they are taken from Department of Defense reports based on Federal income tax withholding reports (W-2 statements). They thus cover actual disbursements classified by state of residence, an important feature in view of the large payrolls in the Washington, D.C., area and other multi-state metropolitan areas.

For 1947-48 and 1954, state estimates were made by distributing national totals to states on the basis of employment shares; residence adjustments were then made for several metropolitan areas on the basis of interpolations and census data on residence and occupation. Some of these distributions and residence adjustments were made by the Office of Business Economics, others by myself.

Prime Contracts

Data on prime contracts by state cover the period after July 1, 1950, by calendar quarter. Because of a strong seasonal pattern in contracting (the second calendar quarter is one of especially high volume), annual totals are preferable to quarterly figures for analysis of changes over several years.

Table 11 shows annual values for work in the United States. The value not reported by state includes work costing less than $10,000, work performed at locations the identity of which is classified information, and intragovernmental contracts negotiated overseas for work in the United States.

Both the Department of Defense contract series and the Office of

TABLE 11. Military Prime Contract Awards for Work in the United States, 1950–62

(Calendar years, millions of dollars)

Year	Total Value	Value Reported by State	Percent Reported by State
1950	10,262	5,648[a]	55.0
1951	39,853	37,738	94.7
1952	37,406	34,532	92.3
1953	22,554	20,829	92.4
1954	13,904	12,720	91.2
1955	16,241	14,672	90.3
1956	21,268	19,576	92.0
1957	18,120	16,534	91.2
1958	24,939	23,040	92.4
1959	23,143	21,111	91.2
1960	23,112	21,039	91.0
1961	26,033	23,661	90.9
1962	28,193	25,371	90.0

Sources: Total Value: U. S. Department of Defense, *Military Prime Contract Awards and Subcontract Payments* (quarterly, 1955–62), plus some unpublished data of the Department. The 1950 figure is partly based on U. S. Department of Defense, *Purchases Under the Armed Services Procurement Act of 1947 in Continental United States, Fiscal Year 1950.* The territories and possessions of the United States are included in the coverage uniformly after 1954; through 1954 the series is not exactly comparable from year to year. All new contracts are included, but additions and deductions from contract amounts are included only if over $10,000 in value. Changes and cancellations are recorded in the period when executed, not the period of the original contract.

Value Reported by State: U. S. Department of Defense, *Military Prime Contract Awards by State* (quarterly, 1950–62); the 1950 and 1951 figures required some estimation based on unpublished data. Alaska and Hawaii amounts are included only for 1956 and later.

[a] Amounts were not classified by state before July 1, 1950.

Business Economics purchases series cover procurement for military equipment, supplies, services, and construction (civil construction by the Army Corps of Engineers is excluded from both). For several reasons, there are large differences between the two in some years. The main reason is the lag of purchases referred to in Chapter V. Another is the margin of error in the compilation of the two series: some small contracts are not reported, and procurement purchases have to be estimated by the Office of Business Economics.

Prime contracts (or "procurement actions") are legal instruments which commit government funds.[3] However, except in the case of pro-

---

[3] A prime contract is one form of "obligation," but the latter term covers other kinds of actions as well. There are considerable differences between the prime contract data and the obligations data which are published in another regular report, the Department of Defense's *Monthly Report on Status of Funds.* Some of these differences are: (1) the functional title classification of obligations is quite different from the claimant program classification of contracts; the

curement of petroleum, contracts which do not specify a firm dollar amount or a fixed quantity (such as open-end, indefinite quantity, or term contracts) are not included in the category, prime contracts, until actual purchase or delivery orders are given.

Classification by State

The notes to the report on contracts by state regularly declare that:

For the majority of the contracts with manufacturers, the data reflect the location of the plant where the product will be finally processed and assembled. Construction contracts are shown for the state where the construction is to be performed. However, for some contracts with large companies with more than one plant, and for contracts with service, wholesale, or other distribution firms, the location is usually the address of the contractor's main office.[4]

Inspection of a sample of contract records on which the series is based suggests that values are usually assigned to the correct state for manufacturing firms, even if the assembly point is not in the state of the head office. Of course, some preliminary work may be farmed out by a company to another plant; this is part of the general problem of allowing for purchases outside the state. However, the use of the state of head office is a definite source of distortion in some service contracts and indefinite-quantity or term contracts.

Importance of Defense Demand in "Defense-Related Industries"

Information on this subject is found in the Census of Manufactures.[5] Some of the information is rather indirect, because for two- and three-digit industries value added but not value of shipments is given, while for four- and five-digit industries, value of shipments but not value added is given.

"operations and maintenance" category of obligations, for example, includes both civilian wages and purchases of certain supplies; (2) obligations are not reported by state; (3) obligations are not shown separately for foreign purchases, while prime contracts are; (4) obligations include "project orders" issued to military-owned and -operated establishments such as Navy yards, while the prime contract series includes these orders only when they are used to cover contracts with business firms; (5) services are not separated from other procurement within a functional title in the obligation series.

[4] U. S. Department of Defense, *Military Prime Contract Awards by State.*

[5] U. S. Bureau of the Census, *U. S. Census of Manufactures: 1958,* Vol. II, Part 2 (1961), Tables 6A in the sections on individual industries; and *U. S. Annual Survey of Manufactures: 1959 and 1960* (1963), Chap. IV; and *U. S. Annual Survey of Manufactures: 1961* (1963), Chap. IV.

In the four-digit industry, 3721, Aircraft, 77 percent, 65 percent, and 51 percent of the "value of work done" was on complete military aircraft in 1954, 1958, and 1961, respectively. Modifications, conversions, overhauls, and research and development are also included in industry 3721; the military portions of these activities were another 18 percent and 15 percent of the total 3721 work done in 1954 and 1958, respectively.

No information is given on the military portion of work in industry 3722, Aircraft Engines and Parts, or in industry 3729, Aircraft Equipment Not Elsewhere Classified. However, of the total value of shipments in these industries, 23 percent, 28 percent, and 40 percent were identified as work on missiles in 1958, 1959, and 1961, respectively. Much more of the work of these industries is of course on military order for ordinary aircraft engines and parts.

The two four-digit industries in SIC 373, Ship and Boat Building and Repairing, are 3731, Ships, and 3732, Boats. Ships is much the larger component, as it comprised 84 percent or more of the total value added in 373 in each of the years 1954, 1958, and 1961. Military production within 3732 is minor, but within 3731, work done on military new construction, repair, and conversion was between 40 and 50 percent of the total in 1954, 1958, and 1961. These figures include only self-propelled military ships.

In SIC 381, the largest five-digit component is 38111, Aircraft Flight Nautical and Navigational Instruments and Automatic Pilots. This component, which presumably is as heavily defense-oriented as the aircraft industry is, accounted for 70 percent or more of the value of shipments of industry 381 in 1954, 1958, and 1961.

Within SIC 366, the largest four-digit industry is Radio and Television Communication Equipment (except home receivers), industry 3662. It accounted for 60 percent or more of the total value added in industry 366 in 1958, 1959, and 1961. Within 3662, in turn, the five-digit industry 36625, Electronic Aircraft and Missile Control, Guidance and Check-Out Systems, accounted for 46 percent and 38 percent of the value of shipments in 1958 and 1961, respectively. Because of the classification change, it is not possible to give military fractions for SIC 366 for earlier years, but the absolute size of industry 36625 in 1954 indicates a sizeable part of SIC 366 was defense production. Within SIC 366 there are large amounts of other defense equipment, for example in industry 36624, Electronic Navigational Aids, and in industry 36626, Other Commercial, Industrial, and Military Electronic Equipment Not Elsewhere Classified.

It is not possible to determine even a rough fraction for activity caused by defense demand in SIC 367.

The following percentages of wages in SIC 371, Motor Vehicles, and 354, Metalworking Machinery, were included in the defense-related group for 1951-53:

	1951	1952	1953
SIC 371	15	30	20
SIC 354	20	40	40

These percentages were determined in the following way: Calendar year amounts of expenditures were estimated from a report of the Department of Defense.[6] In the case of vehicles, these amounts were expressed as approximate fractions of estimated industry product in automobiles and automobile equipment, as estimated from national income data.[7] For production equipment, the amounts were expressed as fractions of total "value of products shipped" for product classes within SIC 354, based on Census of Manufactures data.[8]

[6] U. S. Department of Defense, *Status of Funds by Budget Category, Military Functions, Fiscal Years 1951-1954* (1955).

[7] Industry output was approximated by adding national income originating in the industry, corporate depreciation charges, and indirect business taxes (estimated at 10 percent of national income originating in the industry, the rough proportion for the whole economy), using data in U. S. Office of Business Economics, *U. S. Income and Output,* a supplement to the *Survey of Current Business* (1958), pp. 131, 216.

[8] U. S. Bureau of the Census, *U. S. Annual Survey of Manufactures: 1953* (1955), pp. 96-97.

Inclusion of parts of SIC 354 and 371 in the defense-related group obviously raises the estimated procurement share for states like Michigan, which have a larger share of those two industries' wages than of the other defense-related industries' wages. It lowers the estimate for states like California, on the other hand. It is useful, therefore, to note the sensitivity of results to the proportions of SIC 354 and 371 wages included in the defense-related distribution. For 1952, a year used in later analysis, and assuming β to be .2, elimination of the two industries from the defense-related group entirely (and thus their inclusion in "other manufacturing") would lower Michigan's share in total defense purchases from 7.42 to 6.43 percent (the share of procurement alone would decline relatively more). If only half the indicated proportions were included as defense-related, the fall would be from 7.42 to 7.00 percent of total purchases. The corresponding declines for the whole East North Central Region would be from 24.16 to 22.93 or from 24.16 to 23.64 percent, respectively. California's share would rise from 12.66 to 13.06 or from 12.66 to 12.84 percent, respectively. Changes for states other than California or the East North Central states would be rather small. The exact proportions of the two industries' wages included as defense-related, therefore, is of relatively little importance given the estimating formula used.

Coverage and Classification Changes in the Covered Wages Data

In the appendix to Chapter III, two changes were discussed which affect the continuity of the Bureau of Employment Security (BES) covered wages data used to estimate export income. These data are also the source for the state distribution of defense-related wages, so the changes must be discussed again, this time in terms of their possible effect on the estimates of defense procurement by state.

The change in 1956, it will be remembered, extended coverage to smaller firms in many states. Again, some light on the possible distortions is shed by the size-of-firm distributions in 1959. Even though they do not represent information for 1956, these 1959 data show the general unimportance of small establishments in the defense-related industries, and thus suggest that extending coverage to them in 1956 had little distorting effect. As stated in the appendix to Chapter III, the two relevant size classes are "less than 3 employees" and "4 to 9 employees." For the defense-related industries group (SIC 19, 366, 367, 372, 373, and 381) in the whole nation, only 1.1 percent of January-March 1959 covered wages were earned in establishments in these two size classes. This is not surprising, as these industries require large-scale operations. While this percentage is very small, the effects of the coverage change for the nation as a whole were actually even less important. This is because the 1.1 percent includes wages in plants with eight or nine employees which were covered both before and after the change (only firms with less than eight employees were affected by the coverage changes). Also, the 1.1 percent includes small plant employment in all states in 1959, whereas the 1956 extension applied only to thirty states. On the national level, then, the effects of the 1956 change on the defense-related industries group are small enough to be ignored.

However, it is possible that there were significant increases in coverage in some particular states. This would be true if a state happened to have many small plants even in those industries where small plants are unimportant in the nation as a whole. This possibility cannot be quantified, because there are no data on size of firm classified simultaneously by state and industry. The information discussed in the appendix to Chapter III on the general unimportance of small manufacturing firms in most states does suggest that even this possibility is not very large.

The second change, in 1958, was the adoption of the 1957 Standard Industrial Classification. The effects of this change on the reporting of the regional distribution of defense-related wages were perhaps greater than those of the coverage change in 1956, but they too were probably not significant enough to destroy any major conclusion. The BES special tabulation of the effects of reclassifications, described in the appendix to Chapter III, shows that SIC 372 and 373 were relatively little affected by the classification change, SIC 19 and 381 were moderately affected, and SIC 366 was greatly affected. The only relevant changes, however, are those which affected the defense-related industries as a group. There were large transfers out of SIC 366 into SIC 367, for example, but these had no effect on the regional distribution of total defense-related wages.

The special tabulation shows this: Of the January-March 1958 wages earned in defense-related industries under the *new* SIC, at least 93 percent were earned in establishments also classified in those industries under the *old* SIC; and, of the defense-related wages under the *old* SIC, at least 89 percent were earned in establishments still classified in defense-related industries under the *new* SIC.

Again, there is the possibility that the few transfers which were made were concentrated in particular states, thus affecting those states' shares of defense-related wages. However, any loss in this share by a state, if caused merely by reclassification, would largely show up as an increase in its share of "other manufacturing" wages. As both these shares receive some weight in estimating shares of defense procurement, the net effect on the final estimate is almost certain to be very small. It is surely insignificant compared to the large uncertainties raised by the general method of estimating procurement shares in the first place.

Measurement of National Purchases

Several important characteristics of the defense procurement purchases series for the whole nation should be mentioned, since they constitute particular shortcomings for analysis of short-run impact of defense procurement. Use of this series means that the same shortcomings apply if the purchases by state figures are used for analysis of short-run regional impact. They are, of course, not used in that way here.

While defense production naturally lags behind defense contracting in time, purchases as measured in official statistics lag behind production itself, and thus lag the income and employment effects of defense demand. This fact can lead to errors in interpretation of short-term movements, especially if the level of procurement is changing sharply.

This second lag occurs because the national income and product accounts, from which the series is derived, record goods and services as federal purchases at delivery, not when produced. Production is recorded in "change in business inventories," reflecting raw materials and work-in-process accumulation by contractors. Upon delivery, the increase in government purchases is offset by the reduction in inventories which the business sector reports, so the net change is zero. The production has actually been recorded earlier, but as inventory accumulation, not government purchases.[9]

Accurate measurement of production for government order in any period requires knowledge of the part of business inventory accumulation which represents response to government demand. Present procedures do not call for reporting such fractions.

Tables 5 and 11 show strikingly the lag of purchases behind contracts. Purchases undoubtedly lagged behind production significantly both in the Korean War buildup and in the post-Korean cutback. The gaps between purchases and contracts at the height of the Korean War and during the following cutback, however, were unusually large for a special reason. A substantial part of the 1951-52 orders never actually resulted in production, because the demand they represented far exceeded capacity. In the 1953-54 cutback, some of these orders were cancelled. Since gross placements and cancellations are not shown separately, but are netted, it is not known exactly how much cancellation took place. It must have been considerable, for some states show negative amounts, especially for certain six-month periods in those two years. Michigan, for example, had a net negative figure for all three six-month periods between July 1953 and December 1954. These negative amounts cannot of course be matched by negative purchases, so the cancellations depress the 1953 and 1954 contract totals to an unrealistic degree.

Cross-Classifications by State and Program

For the fiscal years since 1960, information exists on the composition of prime contracts in each state; contract value is classified according to SIC industries for 1960, and according to the Department of Defense "programs" for 1961 and later.[10] (Representative programs are "aircraft," "missiles," "miscellaneous hard goods," and so forth.)

---

[9] The importance of this has been stressed in Murray L. Weidenbaum, *Government Spending: Process and Measurement* (1958).

[10] The material for fiscal year 1960 is in Walter Isard and James Ganschow, *Awards of Prime Military Contracts by County, State and Metropolitan Area of the United States, Fiscal Year 1960* (Regional Science Research Institute, n.d.). It classifies contracts by four-digit SIC titles, based on brief descriptions in official

In my dissertation, the cross-classification for fiscal year 1961 was used to estimate the distribution of procurement by states in a manner which differs from the one described in this chapter. Those alternative results were there compared with a fiscal year 1961 distribution estimated in much the same way as that described here. The reader is referred for detailed results to the earlier version of the book (pp. 118-125); they will be described only briefly here. This special comparison with an alternative method was made only for fiscal year 1961.

The alternative method for fiscal year 1961 included no adjustment for timing, and it employed the assumption that contract totals for each program were accurate measures of national purchases. Each program was then adjusted for dispersion using separate defense-related industries. For example, the electronics program was distributed by giving a weight of .5 to the state shares in the program's prime contracts, a weight of .25 to shares in wages in SIC 366 and 367, and .25 to shares in "other manufacturing," as defined earlier in the text. Other appropriate defense-related industries were used for other procurement programs. The alternative method was thus more detailed than the one used in this book.

The results were compared with fiscal year 1961 estimates whose derivation resembles that of the more highly aggregated estimates generally used in this book (except that the more aggregated procedure did not use a timing adjustment and used a single value of β equal to .2). The comparison showed the general outlines of the two sets of estimates to be rather similar. For no state were the estimated shares more than one percentage point apart, and for many the results were almost exactly the same.

One thing revealed by this comparison was the importance of the assumption one made about contracts listed in the official report as not distributed by state. The general approach used here and described in Chapter V assumes such contracts are geographically distributed exactly like the totals which *are* assigned to states. The alternative procedure for the special comparison, however, distributed them by giving a weight of .5 both to the distribution of military forces and to "other manufacturing." The procedure is plausible if these small contracts are mostly for local supplies bought near military bases. This factor seems to explain

reports for each contract. The cross-classifications for 1962 and later were prepared by the Defense Department; they are published in U. S. Department of Defense, *Military Prime Contract Awards by Region and State, Fiscal Years 1962, 1963, and 1964* (1965). The material for 1961 is unpublished; I used it for the estimates described in the next paragraph of the text.

why the states which showed large differences between the two methods included those with larger shares in the distribution of military personnel (by duty station) than in major procurement contracts, or vice versa. The states of North Dakota, Nebraska, Kentucky, Virginia, North Carolina, South Carolina, Georgia, Alaska, Hawaii, and all four states in the West South Central Region had higher shares under the alternative procedure than under the more general one; the opposite was true for California, New York, and Connecticut.

CHAPTER VI

The Impact of Defense Purchases on Regional Growth

THERE WERE DRAMATIC CHANGES in the regional distribution of defense purchases in the 1950's and early 1960's. The Middle Atlantic Region and the Midwest suffered large losses in both a relative and absolute sense, while the Pacific and Mountain Regions and the state of Florida showed especially large gains. These and other changes were caused mainly by shifts in procurement. The two wage and salary components of purchases changed less dramatically, and in some states, in a direction opposite to changes in procurement.

Table A-1 presents dollar estimates for total purchases for each state and Census region, for each of the years 1951-62. These amounts are the sums of the three components of purchases—military wages and salaries, civilian wages and salaries, and estimated procurement purchases. The procurement estimates are those which employ a value of .2 for β in equation (17). Use of either .1 or .3 instead of .2 would probably not alter the main conclusions in any significant way. The interested reader, however, will find sets of all three alternative estimates for procurement in Table A-2; with the figures for military and civilian payrolls in Tables A-3 and A-4, he can derive the alternative estimates of total purchases.

Table 12 is more selective, in that it shows dollar estimates for total purchases for only twenty-eight states and the nine regions, and for only three representative years, 1952, 1956, and 1962; it also expresses the state amounts as percentages of the national total. Each of the twenty-eight states accounted for at least 1 percent of the national total of purchases in at least one of the three years, which themselves were chosen for the following reasons: The year 1952 is representative of the period of the Korean War, more so than either 1951 or 1953; the level of purchases in 1951 was not yet near the Korean War peak, and while purchases were higher in 1953 than in 1952, the contract distribution in 1953 reflected significant cancellations, a factor which makes it less suitable than 1952.[1] The year 1956 best represents the post-Korean period of lower levels; the total had risen only slightly from the low of 1955, and the 1956 figures are not distorted by the effects of heavy cancellations. The 1955 figures would reflect the cancellations of 1953 and 1954, and those for 1957 the uneven and temporary cutback in aircraft contracting in that year. The year 1962 is the last for which estimates could be made in the way described, and no unusual circumstances in 1962 warrant use of some other recent year.

The conclusions of this chapter are based on the estimates of total purchases by state and the model of regional growth described earlier. Later chapters discuss in more detail the changes over time in the distributions of each of the three components of purchases.

Because the national totals declined between 1952 and 1956, then rose to a new high in 1962, change in a state's percentage share is of course not necessarily even in the same direction as change in its dollar amount. Table 12 shows that percentage shares declined for all eight Middle Atlantic and East North Central states between 1952 and 1962, and that of these, only Michigan and Wisconsin partially regained between 1956 and 1962 the relative share each lost between 1952 and 1956. Shares for Virginia, Florida, Colorado, Utah, and California all increased in both sub-periods. As measured in absolute percentage points, between 1952 and

---

[1] See "Measurement of National Purchases," in the appendix to Chap. V.

TABLE 12. Estimated Defense Purchases for Selected States and All Regions, 1952, 1956, and 1962[a]

(Amounts in millions of dollars)

State or Region	1952 Amount	1952 Percent of U. S.	1956 Amount	1956 Percent of U. S.	1962 Amount	1962 Percent of U. S.
Alabama	441	1.10	470	1.40	579	1.29
California	5,061	12.66	5,412	16.18	7,988	17.86
Colorado	249	.62	318	.95	658	1.47
Connecticut	1,077	2.69	1,137	3.40	1,290	2.88
District of Columbia	403	1.01	346	1.03	374	.84
Florida	515	1.29	639	1.91	1,099	2.46
Georgia	745	1.86	705	2.11	944	2.11
Illinois	2,154	5.39	1,729	5.17	1,718	3.84
Indiana	1,431	3.58	768	2.30	958	2.14
Kansas	489	1.22	653	1.95	654	1.46
Kentucky	418	1.05	308	.92	425	.95
Louisiana	374	.94	342	1.02	440	.98
Maryland	1,062	2.66	1,074	3.21	1,222	2.73
Massachusetts	1,255	3.14	1,010	3.02	1,728	3.86
Michigan	2,967	7.42	894	2.67	1,401	3.13
Missouri	814	2.04	687	2.05	868	1.94
New Jersey	1,918	4.80	1,526	4.56	1,977	4.42
New York	4,318	10.80	3,038	9.08	3,729	8.35
North Carolina	625	1.56	612	1.83	810	1.81
Ohio	2,410	6 03	1,812	5.42	2,101	4.70
Oklahoma	403	1.01	385	1.15	446	1.00
Pennsylvania	2,206	5.52	1,708	5.11	2,191	4.90
South Carolina	410	1.03	340	1.02	465	1.04
Texas	1,773	4.43	1,847	5.52	2,254	5.04
Utah	143	.36	140	.42	448	1.00
Virginia	1,284	3.21	1,122	3.35	1,555	3.48
Washington	1,055	2.64	965	2.88	1,378	3.08
Wisconsin	699	1.75	370	1.11	530	1.18
New England	2,944	7.36	2,668	7.97	3,698	8.27
Middle Atlantic	8,442	21.11	6,272	18.75	7,897	17.65
East North Central	9,660	24.16	5,571	16.65	6,705	14.99
West North Central	2,126	5.32	1,983	5.93	2,570	5.74
South Atlantic	5,295	13.24	5,012	14.98	6,762	15.11
East South Central	1,412	3.53	1,267	3.79	1,713	3.83
West South Central	2,702	6.76	2,722	8.14	3,335	7.45
Mountain	834	2.09	1,064	3.18	1,957	4.37
Pacific	6,305	15.77	6,508	19.45	9,535	21.31
United States	39,983	100.00	33,457	100.00	44,738	100.00

Sources: Calculated from the sources listed for Tables 5 and 11.
[a] Regional amounts do not add to national totals because Alaska and Hawaii are not included in any region.

1962, California increased its share of the national total far more than any other state, and Michigan experienced the greatest decline. The largest relative increases occurred in Florida, Colorado, and Utah, each of which doubled or nearly doubled its share. Over the ten-year period, the Mountain Region more than doubled its percentage share, and experienced the greatest relative change, followed by the Pacific Region, which increased its relative share by about a third (nearly all in California). The relative share of the East North Central Region declined by nearly 40 percent, and that of the Middle Atlantic Region by almost 20 percent.

In many important states, changes in shares were different in the two sub-periods. The initial rise in the importance of aircraft after the Korean War and then its relative decline explain the cases of Connecticut, Kansas, and Texas, for these states did not gain nearly so large a share in the new missiles field as they had had in aircraft. Michigan's tremendous decline after the Korean War reflected drastically reduced purchases of military vehicles, and its modest absolute gain in 1956-62 was due in part to the slightly increased importance of vehicles in the 1960's. (It is also true that the timing adjustment may be at fault in the case of Michigan, for the value of s in 1956 is depressed by the heavy cancellations of 1954 and is considerably below the contract share unadjusted for timing by the moving average.)

The Estimation of Defense Income

The important changes in distribution between 1952 and 1962 have been described. In order to analyze their effect on the growth in personal income, the simple model described in Chapter III is applied to them. The first step is to convert the estimates of defense purchases to the same income basis used in that model. Adjustment is necessary only for procurement, as the other two types of purchases are already on a personal income basis. The adjustment amounts for procurement exclude value added which does not become exogenous personal income; this adjustment can be made only roughly, using data for the nation as a whole. The end result was to include 70 percent of the total procurement (estimated with

$\beta = .2$) as the personal income equivalent,[2] which is called "defense income" here.

It must be noted that the dividends and interest portion of defense value added are treated as if paid to residents of the state where *earned*; no adjustment is made to allow for net outflow of capital income to shareholders and bondholders in other states. Such an adjustment would require a great deal more research, use of unpublished sources, and estimation, but it should be attempted in further research in the field to improve the accuracy of the estimates. This adjustment would probably raise the amounts of defense income in the New England and East North Central Regions

---

[2] The amounts which must be eliminated in converting purchases to personal income are: (1) Capital Consumption Allowances; (2) Indirect Business Taxes; (3) Statistical Discrepancy; (4) Corporate Profits Taxes; (5) Undistributed Corporate Profits; (6) Supplements to Wages and Salaries. The first three are deducted from gross national product to arrive at national income in national accounts (so are business transfer payments, but they are small enough to be ignored). Therefore, all six can be subtracted by multiplying total defense purchases by the following product of two fractions:

$$\frac{\text{National Income}}{\text{Gross National Product}} \cdot \frac{\text{National Income minus Items (4), (5), and (6)}}{\text{National Income}}$$

The first fraction is available only for total manufacturing, not for individual industries. Postwar figures for it can be found in Martin L. Marimont, "GNP by Major Industries," *Survey of Current Business,* Vol. 42 (October 1962), pp. 6-18; and in "GNP by Major Industries, 1958-1962, Revised and Updated," *Survey of Current Business,* Vol. 43 (September 1963), pp. 9-10. The second fraction can be calculated for two-digit industries in manufacturing from data in U. S. Office of Business Economics, *U. S. Income and Output,* a supplement to the *Survey of Current Business* (1958), pp. 131, 200-07; and in "National Income and Product Accounts," *Survey of Current Business,* Vols. 42-43 (July issues, 1962-63), Tables 7 and 50-61.

The product of the two fractions naturally varies from year to year and from industry to industry. For total manufacturing, the product is a little below .70 for most years of the postwar period. For specific industries it was above or below that level. In nonautomotive transportation equipment, a major defense industry, it tended to fluctuate around .75. This seemed to call for a fraction a little higher than for total manufacturing, so the figure of .70 was decided upon. This fraction, then, was used for all states and all three of the representative years employed in the following analysis. In other words, 70 percent of a state's estimated procurement was added to its military and civilian payrolls to derive a "defense income" figure.

This technique is admittedly crude in applying the same fraction to all states, since the industrial structure of the states, including the industrial composition of the defense goods and services produced, varies so widely.

and lower them in all other regions except the Pacific, where the potential net effect seems uncertain.

The Relative Importance of Defense Income

Table 13 presents defense income by state, in dollar amounts and as percentages of total exogenous income, for both the A_1 and the A_3 definitions, for the usual three years. The percentages are referred to as "relative importance percentages." (They are, of course, the same for per capita variables as for total variables.)

Table 13 contains few surprises. There are the expected high percentages for many states in 1952, and the sharp declines by 1956, reflecting post-Korean cutbacks. Certain states—Connecticut, Kansas, Maryland, Virginia, Washington, California, Alaska, and Hawaii—show high values for all three years. The table shows that some states not so important in defense procurement nevertheless depend a great deal on military and civilian payrolls of the defense establishment; these include Rhode Island, South Carolina, Kentucky, Alabama, Mississippi, New Mexico, and Alaska and Hawaii. The table also confirms, of course, that for a number of states, defense income was comparatively unimportant in 1956 and 1962; among these states were Vermont, Iowa, South Dakota, West Virginia, Idaho, and Oregon, for example.[3]

[3] Reference to defense income as a percentage of some measure of exogenous income is not at all common in the usual discussions of the regional impact of defense purchases. More commonly, employment or payrolls in certain industries, such as aircraft and ordnance, and in federal defense installations, are compared to total, or total manufacturing, employment or payrolls. However, George Steiner used the exogenous component approach in analyzing defense purchases in Southern California (eight-county area) for fiscal year 1960. He assumed 80 percent of California's contracts went to this area, and that the dollar amount of contracts sufficiently approximated value added (thus assuming purchases from other states were offset by purchases from California firms by firms in other states). To this he added civilian payrolls and 75 percent of military payrolls (75 percent of payrolls unadjusted for dependents' allotments). This gave total purchases of $4.5 billion. Estimating the ordinary income multiplier at 2.2, he multiplied to get $10 billion, then compared this to an estimated "gross regional product" for Southern California of $30 billion in 1959. The resulting relative importance fraction of one-third is near the 1956 and 1962 figures derived in the present study, using the A_3 definition of exogenous income. See Committee for Economic Development, Southern California Associates, *National Defense and Southern California, 1961-1970* (The Associates, 1961).

TABLE 13. Defense Income in Dollars and as a Percentage of Exogenous Income, by State and Region, 1952, 1956, 1962

(Dollar amounts in millions)

State or Region	1952			1956			1962		
	Dollar Amount	Percent of A_1	Percent of A_3	Dollar Amount	Percent of A_1	Percent of A_3	Dollar Amount	Percent of A_1	Percent of A_3
Maine	135	16.8	19.9	147	16.6	19.7	185	16.6	19.5
New Hampshire	88	17.6	22.4	80	13.5	17.4	149	18.3	23.8
Vermont	43	13.8	17.7	24	7.1	9.2	30	7.2	9.7
Massachusetts	989	19.5	28.2	804	13.6	19.9	1,327	17.0	23.9
Connecticut	769	26.8	37.3	814	23.0	32.9	928	20.3	28.5
Rhode Island	237	25.4	33.7	193	18.7	24.9	218	18.2	24.4
New England	2,257	21.5	31.0	2,065	16.8	24.6	2,834	17.8	25.3
New York	3,225	21.1	27.3	2,315	12.7	16.5	2,802	11.8	14.8
New Jersey	1,459	24.6	41.7	1,168	16.2	27.8	1,517	16.0	26.8
Pennsylvania	1,711	15.8	24.7	1,345	10.6	16.5	1,716	11.2	17.1
Middle Atlantic	6,395	19.9	31.6	4,829	12.7	20.0	6,035	12.4	18.5
Ohio	1,798	19.3	29.2	1,382	12.2	18.9	1,597	11.6	17.0
Indiana	1,055	24.4	36.8	575	11.5	17.8	715	11.1	16.3
Illinois	1,642	16.7	25.7	1,333	11.2	17.6	1,337	8.9	13.3
Michigan	2,133	27.9	40.2	671	7.2	10.5	1,052	9.4	13.2
Wisconsin	512	14.1	20.4	275	6.7	10.1	390	7.4	10.4
East North Central	7,139	20.5	32.6	4,232	10.2	16.5	5,088	9.8	15.0
Minnesota	255	10.4	13.1	197	6.9	9.0	294	7.7	10.1
Iowa	194	7.6	9.0	148	5.9	7.4	209	6.1	8.5
Missouri	620	18.1	25.2	534	13.2	18.9	677	12.7	17.4
North Dakota	14	3.6	3.6	17	3.6	3.6	72	8.6	8.7
South Dakota	43	9.3	10.0	42	8.8	9.4	79	9.7	10.3
Nebraska	123	10.3	10.9	111	10.0	11.1	171	9.8	10.7
Kansas	385	20.0	22.6	512	27.6	31.7	518	20.2	23.0
West North Central	1,635	13.2	16.5	1,565	11.8	15.4	2,022	10.9	14.1
Delaware	94	18.6	24.5	68	9.2	11.6	95	10.4	12.5
Maryland	897	34.6	48.4	912	28.4	39.3	1,046	23.1	30.8
District of Columbia	364	30.0	29.4	324	26.0	24.9	337	20.9	19.5

Virginia	1,200	39.1	46.8	1,060	30.9	38.0	1,409	30.0	37.4
West Virginia	95	6.2	7.2	73	4.5	5.2	127	7.0	8.1
North Carolina	532	18.6	21.8	522	15.2	18.4	690	14.8	18.1
South Carolina	371	25.4	29.5	313	19.1	22.4	420	18.6	22.3
Georgia	644	27.2	33.8	616	22.2	28.6	819	21.5	27.5
Florida	480	22.9	25.8	589	18.5	20.9	926	17.6	20.1
South Atlantic	4,675	26.4	33.8	4,477	21.0	27.4	5,872	19.9	25.6
Kentucky	380	18.9	25.2	276	12.1	17.7	382	12.7	18.1
Tennessee	300	14.5	20.5	259	10.5	15.2	344	10.4	14.8
Alabama	385	20.8	26.7	411	19.1	25.6	509	17.0	21.8
Mississippi	162	14.6	16.8	162	13.9	16.7	248	15.4	18.9
East South Central	1,225	17.4	24.0	1,105	13.7	19.8	1,481	13.5	19.2
Arkansas	132	12.7	14.5	134	11.4	13.4	169	10.8	13.2
Oklahoma	353	21.1	24.7	342	18.7	22.4	402	16.6	19.6
Louisiana	319	17.7	20.6	292	13.7	16.3	370	13.5	15.8
Texas	1,540	24.1	28.9	1,595	21.2	26.4	1,917	18.9	23.3
West South Central	2,343	21.5	25.8	2,364	18.7	23.4	2,859	16.9	21.0
Montana	32	5.6	5.7	41	6.5	6.9	84	10.0	10.5
Idaho	41	8.0	8.4	35	6.5	7.0	54	7.9	8.7
Wyoming	41	14.4	13.8	49	16.0	15.5	57	15.0	14.8
Colorado	229	18.2	22.6	288	19.9	24.9	536	25.2	31.0
Utah	135	23.6	27.4	130	19.5	23.7	356	34.7	41.3
Nevada	36	20.0	17.6	51	22.7	18.5	58	18.3	13.4
Arizona	122	16.6	18.3	206	21.6	24.6	277	19.0	22.2
New Mexico	133	24.5	25.8	158	26.6	28.7	199	23.2	24.8
Mountain	768	16.5	18.6	956	17.8	20.7	1,619	21.0	24.2
Washington	870	35.1	41.8	795	27.9	34.0	1,094	28.0	33.2
Oregon	151	10.3	12.0	107	6.5	7.8	135	6.5	7.7
California	4,162	32.3	41.9	4,353	26.3	35.3	6,277	25.6	33.9
Pacific	5,182	30.8	39.5	5,254	25.0	33.0	7,506	24.6	32.7
Hawaii	125[a]	25.1	25.4	180[b]	30.8	31.3	340	42.0	44.7
Alaska	137[a]	48.8	48.8	187[b]	58.4	59.7	205	60.1	58.7
United States	31,883			27,217			35,858		

Source: Amounts calculated from data in Table 12; percentages calculated on the basis of two estimates of exogenous income (see Chaps. III and IV

[a] Includes only military payrolls.
[b] Includes only military payrolls and estimated procurement.

The reader is reminded of a discrepancy between the industrial composition of exogenous income and that of defense income. The percentage of relative importance has precise meaning only if all defense income is earned in industries included in the E component of A. The methods used here do not insure this, under any of the three definitions. The A_3 definition seems more deficient on this score than A_1, because it may not include even those "defense-related" industries which were used to make the dispersion adjustments described in Chapter V; the location coefficient, in other words, may exclude a defense-related industry from the export sector even though the state's share in that industry influenced its estimate for defense income. This problem is not present with the A_1 definition. However, there is the problem of construction, which is an important form of procurement for some states, but which is not included in the exogenous sector under any definition. These discrepancies have the effect of overstating the percentage of relative importance. One correction would be to use only the A_1 definition, and to add all construction wages to it, to make the maximum correction for the error. But construction is not large enough, even in total, to alter the percentages greatly even for those states where it is an important form of procurement.

Another source of bias does not operate in the same direction for all states. It was mentioned earlier that the defense income estimates, being derived from value added estimates, included property income in the state where it was earned. However, exogenous income, being partly estimated from the personal income statistics, includes property income in the state where it was received. This causes the percentage of relative importance to be overstated for some states and understated for others.

Contribution to Growth

The distinction between growth in defense income and in total exogenous income offers a basis for judgments about the importance of the distribution of defense purchases for regional growth.

Tables 14, 15, and 16 summarize some measures of the contribution of defense income to growth. These measures are described more fully below, but the tables include figures on the growth rate of defense income and exogenous income which are of immediate interest. Tables 14, 15, and 16 cover the 1952-56, the 1956-62,

TABLE 14. Contribution of Defense Income to Growth in Exogenous Income, by State and Region, 1952–56

(In percentages)

State or Region	Annual Rate of Growth, 1952–56			Relative Contribution of Defense Income to Growth	
	Defense Income	Exogenous Income			
		A_1	A_3	A_1	A_3
Maine	2.2	2.5	2.3	15	19
New Hampshire	− 2.4	4.4	4.0	− 10	− 13
Vermont	−13.6	2.2	1.7	− 85	−142
Massachusetts	− 5.0	3.9	3.6	− 25	− 39
Connecticut	1.4	5.3	4.7	7	11
Rhode Island	− 5.0	2.6	2.4	− 49	− 70
New England	− 2.2	4.0	3.6	− 12	− 19
New York	− 8.0	4.6	4.5	− 37	− 49
New Jersey	− 5.4	5.0	4.6	− 27	− 49
Pennsylvania	− 5.8	4.0	4.2	− 23	− 34
Middle Atlantic	− 6.8	4.4	4.5	− 31	− 48
Ohio	− 6.4	5.0	4.3	− 25	− 43
Indiana	−14.1	3.8	3.1	− 91	−167
Illinois	− 5.1	4.7	4.3	− 18	− 30
Michigan	−25.1	5.2	4.8	−135	−210
Wisconsin	−14.4	2.9	2.1	− 70	−140
East North Central	−12.3	4.6	4.0	− 55	−100
Minnesota	− 6.2	3.7	3.1	− 17	− 26
Iowa	− 6.5	− .7	− 1.9	− 71	− 31
Missouri	− 3.8	4.2	3.6	− 16	− 27
North Dakota	5.0	4.7	5.1	4	4
South Dakota	− .6	1.1	.8	− 5	− 8
Nebraska	− 2.5	− 1.8	− 2.9	− 14	− 9
Kansas	7.4	− .9	− 1.3	164	129
West North Central	− 1.1	1.7	.7	− 9	− 26
Delaware	− 7.8	10.2	11.3	− 14	− 17
Maryland	.4	5.5	5.8	3	3
District of Columbia	− 2.9	.7	1.2	−124	− 71
Virginia	− 3.1	2.8	2.2	− 43	− 66
West Virginia	− 6.4	1.5	1.3	− 26	− 35
North Carolina	− .5	4.7	3.9	− 2	− 3
South Carolina	− 4.2	3.0	2.7	− 36	− 46
Georgia	− 1.1	4.0	3.1	− 7	− 12
Florida	5.2	11.0	10.9	11	12
South Atlantic	− 1.1	4.7	4.3	− 6	− 9
Kentucky	− 7.7	3.2	.9	− 45	−216
Tennessee	− 3.6	4.4	3.8	− 12	− 19
Alabama	1.6	3.9	2.7	9	16
Mississippi	0.0	1.3	.2	0	0
East South Central	− 2.6	3.5	2.2	− 13	− 28
Arkansas	.4	3.1	2.4	2	2
Oklahoma	.8	2.3	1.6	− 7	− 12
Louisiana	− 2.2	4.2	3.8	− 9	− 12
Texas	.9	4.1	3.2	5	8
West South Central	.2	3.8	2.8	1	2
Montana	6.4	2.4	1.8	15	20
Idaho	− 3.9	1.2	.8	− 26	− 41
Wyoming	4.6	1.8	1.6	37	40
Colorado	5.9	3.5	3.4	31	39
Utah	− .9	3.8	2.7	− 6	− 9
Nevada	9.1	5.7	7.8	32	21
Arizona	14.0	6.8	5.9	34	43
New Mexico	4.4	2.3	1.3	47	87
Mountain	5.6	3.6	2.8	26	37
Washington	− 2.2	3.6	3.0	− 21	− 31
Oregon	− 8.3	2.9	2.3	− 29	− 43
California	1.1	6.5	5.6	5	8
Pacific	.3	5.7	4.9	2	2
United States	− 3.9				

Source: Calculated from data in Table 12 and from two estimates of exogenous income (see Chaps. III and IV).

91

TABLE 15. Contribution of Defense Income to Growth in Exogenous Income, by State and Region, 1956–62

(In percentages)

State or Region	Annual Rate of Growth, 1956–62			Relative Contribution of Defense Income to Growth	
	Defense Income	Exogenous Income			
		A₁	A₃	A₁	A₃
Maine	3.9	3.9	4.1	17	19
New Hampshire	10.9	5.5	5.3	27	36
Vermont	3.8	3.5	3.0	8	12
Massachusetts	8.7	4.8	5.4	25	32
Connecticut	2.2	4.4	4.7	12	15
Rhode Island	2.1	2.6	2.4	15	22
New England	5.4	4.4	4.9	21	27
New York	3.2	4.5	5.1	9	10
New Jersey	4.5	4.7	5.1	16	25
Pennsylvania	4.1	3.2	3.6	14	19
Middle Atlantic	3.8	4.1	5.2	12	15
Ohio	2.4	3.3	4.3	9	11
Indiana	3.7	4.3	5.2	10	13
Illinois	.1	4.0	4.9	a	a
Michigan	7.8	2.9	3.7	19	22
Wisconsin	6.0	4.5	5.4	9	11
East North Centra	3.1	3.7	4.7	9	11
Minnesota	6.9	5.1	4.9	9	13
Iowa	5.9	5.1	5.1	7	9
Missouri	4.0	4.8	5.5	11	14
North Dakota	27.2	10.3	9.8	10	10
South Dakota	11.1	9.2	9.4	11	11
Nebraska	7.5	7.9	8.0	9	10
Kansas	.2	5.5	5.7	1	1
West North Central	4.4	5.7	6.0	9	11
Delaware	5.7	3.5	4.4	15	15
Maryland	2.3	5.9	6.6	11	14
District of Columbia	.7	4.3	4.9	4	4
Virginia	4.9	5.4	5.1	31	37
West Virginia	9.7	1.7	2.0	26	25
North Carolina	4.8	5.3	5.0	14	18
South Carolina	5.0	5.4	5.1	18	22
Georgia	4.9	5.4	5.6	20	25
Florida	7.8	8.8	8.5	16	19
South Atlantic	4.6	5.6	5.8	17	22
Kentucky	5.6	4.8	5.2	14	19
Tennessee	4.8	5.1	5.4	10	14
Alabama	3.6	5.7	6.5	12	14
Mississippi	7.4	5.5	5.2	19	24
East South Central	5.0	5.2	5.6	13	18
Arkansas	3.9	4.9	4.3	9	13
Oklahoma	2.7	4.7	5.1	11	12
Louisiana	4.0	4.3	4.5	13	14
Texas	3.1	5.1	5.3	13	15
West South Central	3.2	4.9	5.1	12	15
Montana	12.7	4.9	5.0	17	18
Idaho	7.5	4.1	3.7	12	14
Wyoming	2.6	3.7	3.3	11	12
Colorado	10.9	6.6	7.0	33	39
Utah	18.3	7.5	7.8	48	56
Nevada	2.2	5.9	7.8	8	5
Arizona	5.1	7.3	6.8	15	18
New Mexico	3.9	6.3	6.5	16	17
Mountain	9.2	6.2	6.4	26	30
Washington	5.5	5.4	5.9	28	32
Oregon	3.9	4.1	4.1	6	7
California	6.3	6.8	7.0	24	32
Pacific	6.1	6.4	6.3	24	32
United States	4.7				

Source: Same as for Table 14.
a Less than .5 percent.

92

TABLE 16. Contribution of Defense Income to Growth in Exogenous Income, by State and Region, 1952–62

(In percentages)

State or Region	Annual Rate of Growth, 1952–62			Relative Contribution of Defense Income to Growth		
	Defense Income	Exogenous Income		A_1	A_3	A_3 Deflated
		A_1	A_3			
Maine	3.2	3.3	3.4	16	19	17
New Hampshire	5.4	5.1	4.8	19	25	27
Vermont	− 3.5	3.0	2.5	−16	−25	−131
Massachusetts	3.0	4.4	4.7	13	18	12
Connecticut	1.9	4.8	4.7	11	15	1
Rhode Island	− .8	2.6	2.4	− 8	−11	−120
New England	2.3	4.3	4.4	12	16	6
New York	− 1.4	4.5	4.9	− 7	− 8	− 28
New Jersey	.4	4.8	4.9	2	3	− 17
Pennsylvania	a	3.5	3.8	b	b	− 21
Middle Atlantic	− .6	4.2	4.9	− 3	− 4	− 23
Ohio	− 1.2	4.0	4.3	− 6	− 8	− 34
Indiana	− 3.8	4.1	4.4	−23	−32	− 76
Illinois	− 2.0	4.3	4.7	− 8	−11	− 33
Michigan	− 6.8	3.9	4.1	−49	−67	−147
Wisconsin	− 2.7	3.8	4.1	−10	−13	− 39
East North Central	− 3.3	4.1	4.4	−17	−24	− 63
Minnesota	1.4	4.5	4.1	3	4	− 2
Iowa	.7	2.7	2.2	2	3	− 18
Missouri	.9	4.6	4.7	4	5	− 8
North Dakota	17.8	8.1	7.9	8	8	9
South Dakota	6.3	5.9	5.9	10	11	11
Nebraska	3.3	3.9	3.5	9	10	10
Kansas	3.0	2.9	2.8	21	24	27
West North Central	2.1	4.1	3.8	7	9	3
Delaware	.1	6.1	7.1	b	b	− 6
Maryland	1.5	5.7	6.3	9	12	− 2
District of Columbia	− .8	2.8	3.4	− 9	− 7	− 46
Virginia	1.6	4.3	3.9	15	19	− 4
West Virginia	2.9	1.6	1.7	11	12	86
North Carolina	2.6	5.0	4.6	10	12	7
South Carolina	1.2	4.4	4.1	7	9	− 6
Georgia	2.4	4.9	4.6	13	18	8
Florida	6.8	9.7	9.5	15	18	17
South Atlantic	2.3	5.3	5.2	11	15	5
Kentucky	.1	4.2	3.4	b	1	− 27
Tennessee	1.4	4.8	4.7	4	6	− 3
Alabama	2.8	5.0	5.0	12	15	9
Mississippi	4.4	3.8	3.2	17	23	31
East South Central	1.9	4.5	4.2	7	11	2
Arkansas	2.5	4.2	3.5	8	10	6
Oklahoma	1.3	3.8	3.7	7	9	− 5
Louisiana	1.5	4.3	4.2	6	7	− 2
Texas	2.2	4.7	4.4	11	14	6
West South Central	2.0	4.5	4.1	10	13	3
Montana	10.1	3.9	3.7	15	16	25
Idaho	2.8	3.0	2.5	7	9	12
Wyoming	3.3	2.9	2.6	16	18	25
Colorado	8.9	5.4	5.5	30	37	43
Utah	10.2	6.0	5.8	40	48	58
Nevada	4.9	5.8	7.8	17	11	9
Arizona	8.5	7.1	6.4	20	24	27
New Mexico	4.1	4.7	4.5	21	24	22
Mountain	7.7	5.1	5.0	25	29	35
Washington	2.3	4.7	4.7	17	20	9
Oregon	− 1.1	3.6	3.4	− 3	− 4	− 22
California	4.2	6.7	6.4	20	27	22
Pacific	3.8	6.1	5.7	19	23	20
United States	1.2					

Source: Same as for Table 14.
a Less than .05 percent.
b Less than .5 percent.

and the 1952-62 periods, respectively. For each of these periods, they give the rate of growth for defense income and for each of the A_1 and A_3 definitions of exogenous income. In all cases the growth rates are for total, not per capita, variables. The growth rates for per capita variables would naturally be lower algebraically, and could be negative even if the rate for the total were positive; they can be approximated closely by subtracting the rate of growth in population from the figures given. The tables also give the rate of growth for the national total of defense income. In all cases, the growth rates are the conventional geometric average or "compound" rates. Rates are not calculated for Alaska and Hawaii because a complete series for defense income is not available for these two states.

These tables show that exogenous income (either definition) grew at a positive rate for all states in the 1952-62 and 1956-62 periods and for most states in the 1952-56 period. In 1952-56, the usual case is a negative rate for defense income. The important exceptions are Connecticut, Kansas, Texas, Florida, California, and some states of the Mountain Region, for which positive rates reflect the remaining high level of aircraft procurement and the early development of missiles at a time when the other parts of the defense budget were being cut greatly. Only three regions, the Pacific, Mountain, and West South Central, avoided declines in defense income. The negative growth rates which are largest in absolute value are found in the Middle Atlantic and East North Central states, some of the West North Central states, and in Kentucky and Tennessee.

All states showed an increase in defense income between 1956 and 1962. But in states in the Middle Atlantic and East North Central Regions, defense income grew more slowly than did the national total. Thus the states in these two regions were not only relatively hard hit by the post-Korean War cutback, but their defense income grew less rapidly than the national average in the later buildup. In the New England, Mountain, and Pacific Regions, on the other hand, defense income grew faster than the national total in 1956-62; many of the states in these two regions also suffered less than others in the cutback period or actually experienced growth in defense income.

Over the entire 1952-62 period, the annual rate of growth for the total United States defense income was small, 1.2 percent per year. The dispersion around that figure is what would be expected from the two halves of the span: the Middle Atlantic and East North Central Regions showed negative rates of growth, especially substantial in the latter case; the major states which experienced especially large rates of increase were Florida, Colorado, Utah, Arizona, and California.

There is no clear relationship, however, between rates of growth in defense income and rates of growth in exogenous income. That is, low rates—or large negative rates—of growth in defense income are not clearly and consistently associated with low rates for the entire exogenous sector. Some states, such as Michigan, Delaware, and Oregon, which suffered greatly from the defense cutback in 1952-56, show higher rates of growth for A than do states like Kansas, Alabama, and Texas, where defense income actually increased. Similar examples can be found for other periods as well. This point is discussed below in another connection.

The important matters here include not only rates of growth of defense income, but also the *weight* of defense income and the *growth of other parts* of the exogenous sector. The latter, for example, is especially relevant in some of the plains and mountain states, where growth in agricultural income lagged significantly behind growth in defense income, thus preventing the total exogenous sector from growing very rapidly.

The measure of relative contribution presented for each state and region in Tables 14, 15, and 16 is calculated as follows:

$$\text{Relative Contribution} = \frac{\dfrac{D_o}{A_o}\, r_D}{r_A},$$

where: D_o is defense income in the first year of the period (1952 or 1956); A_o is exogenous income in the first year of the period; and r_D and r_A are the annual rates of growth over the period of defense income and of exogenous income, respectively.

This formula simply weights the growth rate in defense income by the importance in the base year, and expresses the result as a percentage of the rate for the whole exogenous sector. In the three tables, the sign of this term is always the sign of r_D, regardless of the sign of r_A. The tables give the measure for both the A_1 and A_3 definitions of exogenous income. The figures for r_D and r_A are from the previous columns of each table, and the figure for D_o/A_o is taken from Table 13. (The final column of Table 16 is described later in the chapter; it is a figure adjusted for inflation.)

Table 14, covering the 1952-56 period, shows measures of relative contribution which clearly demonstrate the severe impact of the post-Korean reductions on some states, including those in the East North Central and Middle Atlantic Regions. The negative numbers indicate a depressing influence on growth which a state had to overcome for any growth in exogenous income to take place. The favorable contributions were large in Maine, Florida, Kansas, and some Mountain states, and they were small but favorable for California, Maryland, Texas, and Connecticut, where aircraft and/or missile production was important.

The measure of relative contribution differs according to which of the two definitions of exogenous income, A_1 or A_3, is used. However, it turns out that the ranking of states by the size of the relative contribution under the A_1 definition is very similar to the one obtained when the A_3 definition is used. Spearman's rank correlation coefficient was calculated for the two different measures in each of the periods analyzed. For the 1952-56 period, the coefficient was .982; for the 1956-62 period, .967; and for the whole 1952-62 period, it was .983. This close similarity in each period of the ranking of the states is a significant result. Although the variations in the definition of exogenous income result in some differences in the absolute size of the measure of the contribution to growth, they result in far less significant differences in the ranking of states according to how they fared.

The approach used here is to estimate the extent to which growth in defense income contributed to growth in exogenous income. At this point, one might pertinently ask what the relationship was between growth in defense income and growth in total personal income, since, as was stressed earlier, the rate of growth of personal income is usually higher than that of exogenous income. One position which seems somewhat defensible is to say that all the growth in personal income was *caused* by growth in exogenous income, even if the two were not the same size. Import substitution, for example, is one factor which makes personal income grow more rapidly than exogenous income, as discussed earlier. One could say that import substitution is possible because the size of the market increases, but that in the last analysis it is possible only if export or other exogenous income grows. In other words, the multiplier is bigger because of import substitution, but there must be something to be multiplied. According to this position, the measures presented here would apply to growth in personal income as well as exogenous income. It is not wise, however, to insist on this point. Some readers may want to adjust the figures (downward, for most states) by multiplying the measures of relative contribution presented here by the ratio between growth rate in exogenous income and growth rate in total personal income, and call the result the proper measure of contribution to growth in personal income. For some states, this adjustment would in fact be sizeable.

Summary Classification of States

In summary, this section gives a cross-classification of states and regions according to the relative importance of defense income in 1962 and according to the relative contribution of defense income to growth in exogenous income.

States are first classified according to the 1962 ratio of defense income to exogenous income. The classification is based on the simple average of the percentages for the A_1 and A_3 definitions. The classes are: "Heavily Dependent on Defense Income," where the average of the two percentages is 25 or greater; "Moderately Dependent," where the average is at least 15 but less than 25 percent; and "Slightly Dependent," where the average is less than 15 percent. Each of these classes is further divided into subcategories defined by the relative role of defense in growth over the entire 1952-62 period. For this purpose, the average of the two measures, one using the A_1 and one the A_3 definition of exogenous income, is again used (the A_3 measure is the one unadjusted for inflation). These subcategories are defined as follows: "Growth Greatly Stimulated," if the average is 20 percent or more; "Growth Moderately Stimulated," if the average is between 10 and 19 percent, inclusive; "Growth Little Affected," if the average is between —9 and +9 percent, inclusive; and "Growth Depressed," if the average is negative and 10 percent or greater in absolute value.

The results of this classification are as follows (Alaska and Hawaii are not classified because of the lack of a continuous series on defense income for them, but they would fall in the "Heavily Dependent" category):

Heavily dependent in 1962:
>   Growth greatly stimulated: Colorado, Utah, California, Pacific Region.
>   Growth moderately stimulated: Maryland, Virginia, Washington.
>   Growth little affected: none.
>   Growth depressed: none.

Moderately dependent in 1962:
>   Growth greatly stimulated: New Hampshire, Kansas, Mississippi, Arizona, New Mexico, Mountain Region.
>   Growth moderately stimulated: Maine, Massachusetts, Connecticut, North Carolina, Georgia, Florida, Alabama, Texas, Nevada, and the New England, South Atlantic, and West South Central Regions.
>   Growth little affected: Rhode Island, New Jersey, Missouri, District of Columbia, South Carolina, Kentucky, Oklahoma, and the Middle Atlantic and East South Central Regions.
>   Growth depressed: none.

Slightly dependent in 1962:
>   Growth greatly stimulated: none.
>   Growth moderately stimulated: South Dakota, West Virginia, Montana, Wyoming.
>   Growth little affected: New York, Pennsylvania, Ohio, Illinois, Minnesota, Iowa, North Dakota, Nebraska, Delaware, Tennessee, Arkansas, Louisiana, Idaho, Oregon, West North Central Region.
>   Growth depressed: Vermont, Indiana, Michigan, Wisconsin, East North Central Region.

Maps 2 and 3 convey this same information.

The lack of a close relationship between the rate of growth of a state's defense income and the rate of growth attained by its exogenous sector was noted earlier. The measure of relative contribution to growth is also not closely related to the rate of growth of exogenous income, either during the whole 1952-62 period, or the two sub-periods. The *relative* contribution to growth of defense income

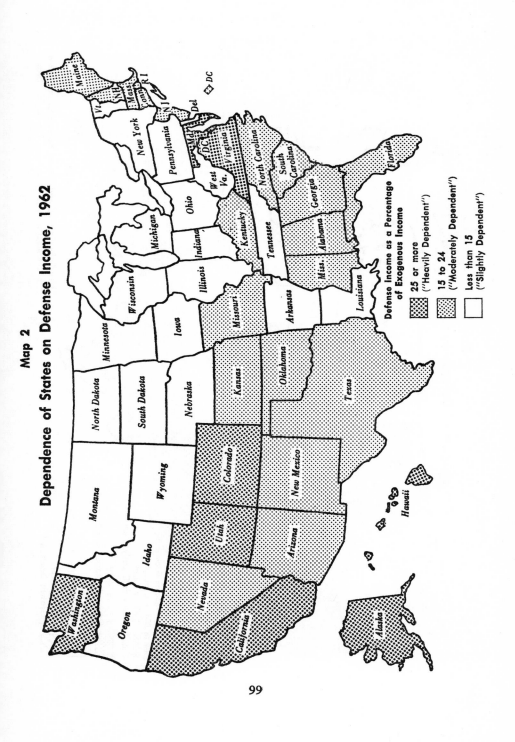

Map 2

Dependence of States on Defense Income, 1962

Defense Income as a Percentage
of Exogenous Income

25 or more
("Heavily Dependent")

15 to 24
("Moderately Dependent")

Less than 15
("Slightly Dependent")

Map 3

Contribution of Defense Income to Growth, 1952-1962 [b/]

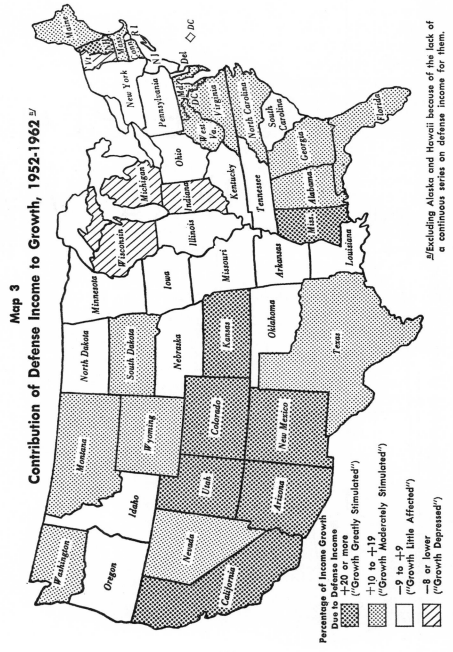

Percentage of Income Growth Due to Defense Income

+20 or more ("Growth Greatly Stimulated")

+10 to +19 ("Growth Moderately Stimulated")

−9 to +9 ("Growth Little Affected")

−8 or lower ("Growth Depressed")

[b/]Excluding Alaska and Hawaii because of the lack of a continuous series on defense income for them.

100

may be great simply because other exogenous income is growing slowly. On the other hand, some states with rapidly growing personal income can be said to have received relatively little stimulus specifically from defense income. Defense income is obviously only one source of growth for an area; even when it is growing rapidly, defense income may not constitute a relatively important factor in general growth, or it can be offset by other factors which retard general growth.

Despite the lack of a strong relationship between the two rates of growth, it may seem reasonable to some to make the following sort of statement: *Ceteris paribus,* whether the rate of growth in exogenous income was high or low, it would have been higher had defense income grown more rapidly or declined less rapidly than it actually did. This is probably not true, however, for all states. In many cases production for defense demand must have used capacity that otherwise would have found employment in some other export industry. In other words, defense production replaced other production and did not really cause the rate of growth in exogenous income to be higher than it would otherwise have been. In such cases, the measure of relative contribution to growth can be interpreted as a sort of measure of the specialization of a state's growth.

On the other hand, the condition, *ceteris paribus,* surely applies to many other states. It seems highly doubtful, for example, that some of the mountain states would have grown as rapidly as they did without the shifts in defense demand. And the generally high unemployment rates and excess capacity in some old-line industrial states suggest that these states would have grown more rapidly had their exports of defense goods—or any other kind—grown more rapidly; in such instances, defense production did not so much replace other production as add a net stimulus.

Unfortunately, this study cannot include the detailed, difficult analysis necessary to classify each state into one group or the other. The question, however, is extremely important and should be investigated, because the answer to it would shed light on the prospects for the successful adjustment of states to any future large cuts, or shifts, in defense demand.

Different Responses to Different Exogenous Income

The high level of aggregation used in the simple model of regional income growth means that the measures of relative importance and contribution to growth can be only approximations. For it may be that the multiplier response of the local sector—and thus of total personal income—is not uniform with respect to all kinds of exogenous income. The $h(Y_p)$ function, which is for total spending minus imports, is an average of many different responses. A more detailed model—an input-output model, for example—would disaggregate both Y_h and A, including within E. Instead of containing only a single function, it would separate the response to export of aircraft, for example, from the response to the export of pulp and paper.

The simple percentages calculated here are misleading if the response of the local sector to defense income is different from the response to other export income, to non-defense property income, or to transfer payments. In those cases, the percentage of total exogenous income does not accurately show the importance of defense income. It is likely that some such differences exist. They can be illustrated by considering the four types of expenditure which determine income in the local sector—consumption, induced local investment, imports, and state and local government.

Two points can be made about consumption. First, the marginal propensity to consume out of defense income may differ from that for other income. Enlisted military personnel may save more relative to other income receivers because they may have fewer opportunities for consumption, or because they may have definite plans for family formation and/or purchase of housing or major durables after leaving active duty (and thus after leaving the state where the defense income was received). Such savings are not necessarily wholly reflected in adjustments in dependents' allotments. Second, the average civilian employee of the Defense Department has a higher income than the average employee in the rest of the economy, so his savings may be correspondingly greater.

The effects on investment of defense purchases will depend upon marginal capital requirements and upon existing capacity. If firms can fill defense orders without expansion of plant, the effect on construction will be less than if new plant is required. If new defense employment opportunities induce in-migration of population, housing investment and state and local government expenditures may be required. Because defense production may differ from the area's traditional manufacturing industry in its requirement for personnel, structures, and social overhead capital and services, defense purchases may have a greater multiplier effect than would a mere increase in production of older industries. This possibility is reinforced by the radical change in procurement after Korea. It would seem to be especially important when defense purchases increase suddenly in an area where they were previously not great; the rapid increases in Florida and some of the Mountain states may have had a greater multiplier effect than non-defense demand.

Some of these causes of higher-than-average multiplier effects may also, however, cause higher-than-average leakages through imports. The need for greater investment may generate more construction, for example, but lack of diversified manufacturing in the area may also force higher imports of materials and fixtures, at least until the market grows large enough to induce new capacity.

The importation of parts and materials by *defense contractors* is *not* a factor which reduces the response in the local sector. Estimated defense procurement is on a value-added basis, and direct import requirements are allowed for by reducing final demand itself directly, and not through the function relating imports to income.

One final consideration is an additional possibility that the contribution of defense income is underestimated. Some industries which do not produce for defense demand and which are treated as exogenous for a state may have located in that state because of the prior existence of defense industries. External economies, for example, may be created by defense industries. The model treats these nondefense industries as exogenous, but in a cause-and-effect sense, defense income may be partly responsible for their growth; this effect is not reflected in the measures of the contribution of defense income to growth in total exogenous income.

The broad question of whether defense income causes responses in local income which are significantly different from those caused by other forms of exogenous income would seem to be a profitable area for further research into the economic impacts of defense.

Defense Income and Other Sources of Growth

The growth, or lack of it, in defense income was only one of many influences on differential regional growth in the period discussed in this study. The measures of relative contribution to growth, presented earlier, quantify only this single influence. The overall influence of the defense shifts relative to the other forces remains to be discussed. The question is: Did other forces tend to reinforce or offset the effects of defense income?

A large positive number for the estimate of growth contribution in a state indicates that the state relied on defense income for a great deal of whatever growth did occur. Over the 1952-62 period as a whole, no state depended entirely—or even nearly entirely—on defense income for growth. Although the estimates automatically include the multiplier effect, the highest positive figure is 48 percent, for Utah; even in the 1956-62 period, when the national total of defense income was growing rapidly, the highest figure is 56 percent for the same state.

A large negative number, on the other hand, indicates a significant depressing influence which had to be more than offset by other forces for a state's economy to grow at all. In the 1952-62 period, no state was so depressed by loss of defense income that it failed to grow at a fairly respectable pace.

Various correlations were run, using each state as an observation, to discover the relationship between the impact of defense and the total growth in personal income. The results of these tests imply a positive, but not strong, relationship between defense income and growth in total personal income, and a positive but even weaker relationship between defense income and per capita personal income. In other words, there was some tendency for states which benefitted greatly from defense shifts to experience rapid growth in personal income, but there was almost no systematic tendency for such states to experience the fastest growth in per capita personal income. The effect defense shifts had, then, was mostly to increase total activity in certain states and at the same time induce differential population growth.

The results of the various correlations were as follows: In each case, growth rates are for the 1952-62 period; there are forty-nine observations, for forty-eight states (all but Alaska and Hawaii) and the District of Columbia; also, in each case, the variables relating to defense impact are on the basis of total, not per capita, defense income. The first point is that the correlations between rate of growth in defense income and the rate for exogenous income are low. As noted above in general terms, the correlation coefficient is .55 if the A_1 definition of exogenous income is used and .46 if the A_3 definition is used. Second, the coefficient of correlation between the rate of growth of defense income and that of personal income is .50 if total personal income is used, and .37 if per capita personal income is used. But these correlations do not use a weighted defense income rate of growth. If the growth rate for defense income is multiplied by the weight of defense income in exogenous income in 1952, the figure which results is a measure of *absolute* contribution to growth. It is measured in average percent growth per year, and is of course the *numerator* of the relative contribution fraction used throughout. This new number was calculated separately for the A_1 and the A_3 definitions of exogenous income, and a simple average was taken of the two. This new variable measuring absolute contribution to growth was correlated with the rates of growth in personal income. The resulting coefficient of correlation is .57 for total personal income and only .19 for per capita personal income. This indicates that states with large absolute benefits from defense income tended to grow more rapidly in general, but that this tendency was not very strong and that the effects on per capita income were largely offset by population growth.

Finally, correlations were run between the income rates of growth and the measures of *relative* contribution to growth from defense income. In other words, the whole fraction was used as a "contribution" variable, not just the numerator. In this case the tests were conducted separately for the two definitions of A, rather than for an average. When this fraction was correlated with personal income growth rate, the coefficient of correlation was .40 for the A_1 definition and .36 for A_3. As expected, both coefficients were lower when per capita income growth rates were used; they were .15 for the A_1 definition and .16 for A_3.

A related question is whether the differences in defense income growth from state to state had the effect of widening or of narrowing the regional income differentials within the nation. Some rank correlations are useful in approaching this problem. Spearman rank correlation coefficients were calculated to compare the 1952 ranking of states by income with their ranking by other variables. The result was that there seems to have been a slight tendency for states with low 1952 ranks in income, total or per capita, to have received the most favorable benefits from defense income. For example, the rank correlation coefficient between personal income in 1952 and rate of growth in defense income, 1952-62, is —.50 if total personal income is ranked and —.28 if per capita income is used (the defense income figure is total, not per capita). The negative values indicate the tendency just described. Since the tendency was quite weak, the specific influence of defense income in narrowing income differentials was probably small.

Use of a weighted defense income growth is more meaningful, however. If the ranking in 1952-62 of absolute contributions to growth, as defined just above (once again, an average of the A_1 and A_3 measures is the variable used), is compared with 1952 income ranks, the coefficient is —.28 for personal income and —.22 for per capita income. The weighted results are lower in absolute value than the unweighted results, partly because some of the highest growth rates in defense income occurred in states with comparatively low total income, and in which defense income was not very large relative to exogenous income. The coefficients for per capita income are a little lower in absolute value than those for total income, partly because some large benefits from defense accrued to states with low ranks in total income but much higher ranks in per capita income, their small total income being matched by small populations.

Over the whole 1952-62 period, there was relatively little change in the ranking of states by per capita income and not very much change in the relative dispersion of incomes. The effect of the pattern of defense income growth was either too small to have an appreciable result, or else was offset by other factors, including, of course, population growth in the states favorably affected. That there was little change in ranking is shown by a comparison of the 1952 ranks and 1962 ranks in per capita income using the rank correlation coefficient; it is .95, and would be even higher if income had not been abnormally low in 1952 in some agricultural states and especially high in those states in 1962. That the dispersion decreased only a little is shown by the coefficient of variation (standard deviation divided by the mean); in 1952 it was .23, and in 1962 it was .21. These coefficients of variation are unweighted; that is, each state's per capita income is weighted equally and the mean value is the mean of these state values, not per capita income for the nation as a whole.

Adjustments for Population Change and Inflation

The measures of "relative contribution" discussed so far have used variables not deflated for population growth or inflation. These variables are not exactly appropriate, and must be adjusted, if one desires measures of contribution to per capita and/or to "real" exogenous income. Either of the adjustments can be described as "deflation"—deflation by population or by a price index as the case may be. The variables must be deflated or divided by the product of population and the price index, if one wishes to analyze real *and* per capita growth. Such deflation has the following effects, assuming the same deflator is used for both defense income and exogenous income: (1) If defense income, exogenous income, and the deflating variable all grew positively in the period, and if defense income grew less rapidly than exogenous income, the adjustment will *reduce* the measure of contribution to growth. (2) If all grew positively, but defense income grew more rapidly than exogenous income, the adjustment will *increase* the measure of contribution to growth.

These effects can be demonstrated by simple algebra, and so can the results of cases with negative growth. The cases described here can be comprehended by remembering that the deflation adjustment leaves unchanged the ratio D_o/A_o, while it is approximately the same as subtracting the same amount from the numerator as from the denominator of the fraction r_D/r_A. If this second fraction is below unity to start with, its value is therefore reduced; if it is above unity to start with, its value is raised.

Primarily for illustration, the measures for the 1952-62 period under the A_3 definition of exogenous income were adjusted for price inflation, but not for population growth; these adjusted measures appear in the last column of Table 16. The Department of Commerce implicit price index for total GNP[4] was used to deflate both defense income and exogenous income (note that an alternative is to deflate defense income by the deflator for the government purchases component of GNP). Between 1952 and 1962, this price index grew 1.8 percent per year, on the average, so the adjustment could be approximated (although it was in fact calculated more exactly) by subtracting 1.8 from both the numerator and denominator of r_D/r_A and then making the usual calculation.

For most states, the adjusted figure for relative contribution to growth is lower than the unadjusted figure for A_3, because in the period 1952-62, defense income in most states grew more slowly than exogenous income as a whole. It is especially noteworthy that the negative figures are lowered *algebraically,* and thus become quite a bit larger in absolute value. The Spearman rank correlation coefficient was also calculated for these two rankings of the relative contribution—the unadjusted rank for the A_3 definition compared to the adjusted rank for the same definition. In this case the coefficient of .893 is still large, although not as large as when unadjusted rankings under alternative definitions of exogenous income were compared earlier. So while deflation changes the values of the relative contributions substantially, it has far less effect upon the rankings of states.

Impact of a Hypothetical Redistribution

The analysis so far has concerned itself with the impact of defense purchases on regional growth. And the derived measures presented so far have implicitly assumed the alternative to defense income is no income at all. Now, as a final exercise, estimates are made of the static redistribution of personal income which would occur if the actual 1962 distribution of defense income were replaced with a regional distribution proportional to population in 1962.

This set of calculations can be easily described. First, each state and region is assumed to receive defense income in proportion to its share of population. The 1962 total of defense income in the nation is distributed according to states' shares of population as of the

[4] "National Income and Product Accounts," *Survey of Current Business,* Vol. 43 (July 1963), p. 14.

middle of 1962. The actual defense income (as estimated in this study) is subtracted from the hypothetical amount, giving the net redistribution to each state and region. A positive amount indicates the hypothetical redistribution would give the state more defense income than it actually received; a negative amount indicates the opposite would be true.

These positive and negative amounts, following the simple model used all along, are changes in exogenous income and are thus multiplied into larger changes in personal income. For these purposes, the A_1 definition of exogenous income is used; the multipliers are usually, but not always, lower than the multipliers for the A_2 or A_3 definitions, thus the estimates are conservative. The change in exogenous income from the redistribution is multiplied by the personal income multiplier, which is $1/(1-h)$, where the value of h is the estimate obtained from the regression equation (7) using the A_1 definition of exogenous income. This gives the predicted change in personal income for each state, which is then expressed as a percentage of total personal income in each state in 1962.

The resulting figures are presented in Table 17. The reader may be surprised at the smallness of the figures for many states, especially the heavily industrial ones in the Middle Atlantic and East North Central Regions. As one might have predicted, the largest negative figures are for Hawaii, Alaska, Utah, Virginia, and Washington.

Of course, these calculations could apply to a hypothetical distribution of some kind of exogenous income other than defense income. The figures could estimate the effects, that is, not of a redistribution of defense income, but of the replacement of defense income by income caused by an alternative set of exogenous demands, such as those which might result from disarmament.

This sort of analysis has some obvious limitations, of course. The distribution of the alternative demand was here assumed to be like that of population, but it may not be. For one thing, the 1962 distribution of population reflected in part the effect of defense demand itself; areas suitable to defense production may not be suitable to alternative production despite having sizeable populations and labor forces. For another, the size of the multiplier is certainly not as large for a downward movement of exogenous income as it is for an upward movement, because of a ratchet effect on consumption and state and local government expenditure, and because of

TABLE 17. Percentage Changes in Personal Income Resulting from a Hypothetical Redistribution of Defense Income, 1962

State or Region	Percentage Change in Personal Income	State or Region	Percentage Change in Personal Income
Maine	a	Kentucky	8
New Hampshire	— 4	Tennessee	12
Vermont	12	Alabama	5
Massachusetts	— 4	Mississippi	13
Connecticut	—10	East South Central	9
Rhode Island	— 5		
New England	— 5		
		Arkansas	12
		Oklahoma	3
New York	2	Louisiana	12
New Jersey	— 3	Texas	a
Pennsylvania	3	West South Central	4
Middle Atlantic	2		
		Montana	6
Ohio	3	Idaho	14
Indiana	3	Wyoming	2
Illinois	4	Colorado	— 9
Michigan	5	Utah	—17
Wisconsin	8	Nevada	3
East North Central	4	Arizona	1
		New Mexico	— 1
		Mountain	— 3
Minnesota	11		
Iowa	10		
Missouri	3	Washington	—13
North Dakota	4	Oregon	10
South Dakota	6	California	—11
Nebraska	6	Pacific	—10
Kansas	— 4		
West North Central	6	Hawaii	—29
		Alaska	—43
Delaware	— 1		
Maryland	— 9		
District of Columbia	—10		
Virginia	—13		
West Virginia	15		
North Carolina	5		
South Carolina	3		
Georgia	— 1		
Florida	2		
South Atlantic	— 2		

Source: Calculated from Table 13 and from data of the Office of Business Economics.
a Less than .5 percent.

110

the lack of a counterpart in the downward movement to the accelerator in the upward. The negative figures, therefore, are too large in absolute value.

Finally, there is the major shortcoming of the simple model employed throughout the study: It is a very partial model and it does not reflect the tight interrelatedness of regions in the economy. The exogenous sector of one region is surely not, in general, independent of the exogenous sectors in other states. An analysis of the regional impact of defense purchases allowing for these interactions must await the availability of data on interregional trading patterns.

Some may feel that the minority of very large negative figures in Table 17 shows that the economic problems raised by disarmament will be relatively small. But this is not necessarily a correct appraisal. Even small declines in personal income mean a sizeable departure from the long-term growth path for a region. And whether the declines will be only temporary depends upon the policies designed to cope with disarmament and upon the natural lags between policy changes and economic responses. Perhaps most important is the uncertainty about the alternative distribution of demand which would arise with disarmament. Some areas would be hurt immensely and for a long time if their specialized resources could find no employment in the new situation. The experience of depressed areas and declining industries even in a growing economy should be enough to insure that possibility.

CHAPTER VII

The Regional Distribution of Procurement

THIS AND THE NEXT CHAPTER contain a closer examination of each of the three types of defense purchases. The regional distributions of each are different, and changes in the three have not always been in the same direction. A look at procurement alone is especially important, for changes in it have been most significant for the distribution of total purchases. This is so, because procurement is much the largest of the three, and because changes in its distribution have been larger and more dramatic than in the two kinds of payrolls.

Geographical Concentration of Procurement

All three distributions given weights in the estimation of procurement—contracts, defense-related wages, and other manufacturing wages—are rather concentrated geographically, and the weighted average estimates of value added are also concentrated. Yet it is interesting that concentration in certain senses has not changed much over the period, despite radical changes in the shares of many states.

Table 18 shows the total shares in the various distributions of the top four, top eight, and top fifteen states, for the three years, 1952, 1956, and 1962. (It also shows the concentration of total estimated purchases, including all three kinds of purchases.) The table demonstrates that concentration of estimated procurement purchases has declined very slightly during the 1952-62 period.

Compared to prime contract shares, the dispersion adjustments reduce concentration of estimated value added only slightly. This is true for all three values of β. In fact, variation of β makes for little difference in concentration, which declines only a little as β is decreased.

Variation in β does affect the relative ranking of individual states, but has little effect upon the composition of the top fifteen as a group. Table 18 lists the top four and second four states. For 1952, the top eight are the same regardless of β, with slight changes in ranking in the second four only. The 1956 result is much the same, with only one change in membership in the top eight when β goes as low as .1. There are more changes in 1962 as β changes, but they are not extreme.

Varying the weight for defense-related wages produces slight change in concentration because most states with large shares of contracts are also industrialized and diversified in structure. Their shares in other manufacturing, while perhaps smaller than in defense-related manufacturing and in contracts, are nevertheless large and contribute much to v even when β is large. This is apparent in the first part of Table 18, where the top eight states in each distribution are listed. Another way of saying this is that states such as California, New York, New Jersey, and Ohio have enough capacity in both defense-related and more general manufacturing to satisfy many of the subcontracting needs of prime contractors located there.

The last part of Table 18 shows that there has been a slight decline in the concentration ratios for total purchases, including payrolls in addition to estimated procurement.

Other Aspects of Concentration

Cross-classifications of contracts by state and program (described in the appendix to Chapter V) reveal other interesting things

TABLE 18. Geographical Concentration of Various Distributions of Defense Purchases, 1952, 1956, and 1962

States	1952	1956	1962
	Percentage of prime contract awards (variable s)		
Top four states	46.8	45.5	43.6
	(N.Y., Calif., Mich., Ohio)	(Calif., N.Y., Conn., Ohio)	(Calif., N.Y., Mass., Conn.)
Top eight states	65.8	64.8	61.1
	(N.J., Ind., Ill., Penna.)	(N.J., Texas, Ill., Penna.)	(Ohio, N.J., Texas, Wash.)
Top fifteen states	85.6	83.7	77.9
Lowest ten states	0.7	0.9	1.5
	Percentage of wages in defense-related industries (variable d)		
Top four states	44.3	49.4	49.2
	(Calif., N.Y., Mich., N.J.)	(Calif., N.Y., N.J., Ill.)	(Calif., N.Y., N.J., Conn.)
Top eight states	68.4	68.8	67.4
	(Ill., Ohio, Ind., Conn.)	(Ohio, Conn., Ind., Penna.)	(Mass., Ill., Ohio, Wash.)
Top fifteen states	89.6	90.5	86.6
Lowest ten states	0.2	0.1	0.1
	Percentage of wages in other manufacturing industries (variable m)		
Top four states	39.5	38.6	36.3
	(N.Y., Penna., Ohio, Ill.)	(N.Y., Penna., Ohio, Mich.)	(N.Y., Penna., Ohio, Ill.)
Top eight states	62.4	62.2	60.4
	(Mich., Calif., N.J., Mass.)	(Ill., Calif., N.J., Mass.)	(Mich., Calif., N.J., Ind.)
Top fifteen states	80.0	79.8	78.5
Lowest ten states	1.0	1.0	0.8
	Percentage of estimated procurement purchases (variable v) with $\beta = .30$		
Top four states	43.4	43.0	42.2
	(N.Y., Calif., Mich., Ohio)	(Calif., N.Y., Ohio, Ill.)	(Calif., N.Y., N.J., Ohio)
Top eight states	65.8	64.0	60.0
	(Ill., N.J., Penna., Ind.)	(N.J., Conn., Penna., Texas)	(Penna., Mass., Conn., Texas, and Ill., tie)
Top fifteen states	85.1	83.8	79.6
Lowest ten states	0.8	0.8	1.4

114

TABLE 18—Continued

States	1952	1956	1962
	with $\beta = .20$		
Top four states	42.4	41.8	40.8
	(N.Y., Calif.,	(Calif., N.Y.,	(Calif., N.Y.,
	Mich., Ohio)	Ohio, Ill.)	Ohio, Penna.)
Top eight states	65.2	62.5	58.8
	(Ill., Penna.,	(Penna., N.J.,	(N.J., Mass.,
	N.J., Ind.)	Conn., Texas)	Ill., Conn.)
Top fifteen states	84.2	82.5	78.6
Lowest ten states	0.8	1.0	1.4
	with $\beta = .10$		
Top four states	41.5	40.6	39.7
	(N.Y., Calif.,	(Calif., N Y.,	(Calif., N.Y.,
	Mich., Ohio)	Ohio, Ill.)	Ohio, Penna.)
Top eight states	64.5	61.6	58.5
	(Penna., Ill.,	(Penna., N.J.,	(N.J., Ill.,
	N.J., Ind.)	Conn., Mich.)	Mich., Mass.)
Top fifteen states	83.2	81.2	77.5
Lowest ten states	0.8	1.1	1.5
Concentration of estimated total defense purchases, including procurement and payrolls (procurement portion estimated with $\beta = .2$). Percentage in:			
Top four states	36.9	36.2	36.1
	(Calif., N.Y.,	(Calif., N.Y.,	(Calif., N.Y.,
	Mich., Ohio)	Texas, Ohio)	Texas, Penna.)
Top eight states	57.0	54.4	52.9
	(Penna., Ill.,	(Ill., Penna.,	(Ohio, N.J.,
	N.J., Texas)	N.J., Conn.)	Mass., Ill.)
Top fifteen states	77.0	74.0	72.8
Lowest ten states	1.6	1.7	2.2

Source: Calculated from Tables 12 and A-2 and from data of the Office of the Secretary of Defense, Bureau of Employment Security, and Office of Business Economics.

about the geographic distribution of procurement contracts. First, in certain individual procurement programs, contracts are even more concentrated than they are in total. Second, research and development contracts are more concentrated than total contracts, both in national total and within programs. A state's share in research and development contracts may be quite different from its share in the value of all contracts; some states received large production contracts in recent years but only small awards for research and development.[1] For example, in fiscal year 1964, the top four

[1] Some of the statements in this section are based on data for fiscal year 1964 in U. S. Department of Defense, *Military Prime Contract Awards by Region and State, Fiscal Years 1962, 1963, and 1964* (1965). Detailed analysis, with various

states had about 42 percent of all contracts, but 59 percent of all research and development awards. In the aircraft program for fiscal year 1961, a special tabulation showed that the top four states had 55 percent of all contracts, but in research and development the top four states had 80 percent; in missiles, the equivalent figures were 69 and 77 percent; in ships, 59 and 90 percent. The top four states are not, of course, the same in all these programs.

Some procurement programs are more closely concerned with research and development than others. In fiscal year 1964, over 20 percent of all price contracts were designated research and development. In missiles alone, the figure was nearly 56 percent. In electronics, it was about 22 percent. This contrasts with 11 percent for aircraft, 10 percent for ships, 3 percent for tank-automotive, 19 percent for weapons, and 12 percent for ammunition.[2] In general, geographical areas which specialize in certain programs are likely to have a higher than average proportion of their contracts in research and development. Moreover, even though certain areas may currently have very heavy production contracts, prospects for the future are diminished if these contracts are part of a program which requires relatively little research and development.[3]

It is perhaps potentially even more distressing to some areas that their eggs are in a very few baskets—that their contracts are concentrated in one or two programs. In fiscal year 1964, missiles accounted for 86 percent and 76 percent of all awards in Utah and Colorado, respectively, and 47 percent in California. Aircraft accounted for 70 percent, 84 percent, 56 percent, and 85 percent, in Kansas, Georgia, Connecticut, and Missouri, respectively.[4] The same is true of construction; in some recent years ICBM base construction and related procurement accounted for the bulk of all procurement of over $10,000 in Arkansas, South Dakota, and

---

concentration ratios for individual programs for fiscal year 1961, based on unpublished data, can be found in my dissertation.

[2] U. S. Department of Defense, *Military Prime Contract Awards and Subcontract Payments* (June 1965).

[3] Examples of such areas, using fiscal year 1961 data, can be found in my dissertation. The possible importance of research contracts for later production contracts is stressed in U. S. Department of Defense, *The Changing Patterns of Defense Procurement* (1962), pp. 7-8.

[4] U. S. Department of Defense, *Military Prime Contract Awards by Region and State, Fiscal Years 1962, 1963, and 1964* (1965).

Wyoming,[5] and construction has in many years of the postwar period been the major part of military procurement in Alaska.

Not only are some states heavily dependent on one or two programs, but in several cases this amounts to dependence on one or two companies. Examples are the Martin-Marietta Company in Colorado; United Aircraft and General Dynamics (Electric Boat Division) in Connecticut; Lockheed in Georgia; Boeing Company in Kansas and Washington; Bath Iron Works in Maine; Ingalls Shipbuilding Company in Mississippi; McDonnell Aircraft in Missouri; and Newport News Shipbuilding and Dry Dock Company in Virginia. In such cases, apprehension about the effects of dependence of certain states and metropolitan areas on defense business is understandable, for these areas may suffer a great loss in demand even if the total defense budget is not cut.

Historical Changes in the Regional Distribution

Table 19 shows the estimated procurement shares for certain states for each of the years 1952, 1956, and 1962. The states included are all those which had 1 percent or more of total procurement in either of the three years. Tables 20, 21, and 22 show the changes in the percentage shares between 1952 and 1956, 1956 and 1962, and 1952 and 1962, respectively, and they also break down the changes into those caused by changes in contract shares and those caused by changes in shares of the two kinds of manufacturing wages.

Most significant were the relative rise of California and the decline of New York and the East North Central states. (These shifts were mainly due to changes in the program composition of procurement, discussed below.) California has long been extremely important in defense procurement, mostly due to its aircraft manufacturers, who also were quick to develop missiles when the latter became important. It ranked second to New York in the Korean War. After the war, purchases of ordnance, vehicles, ammunition, and production equipment were drastically cut, but those of aircraft were sustained. California's share thus rose sharply in 1954 and has since remained larger than that of any other state. The difference

[5] *Ibid.*, and *Air Force Intercontinental Ballistic Missile Construction Program*, Hearing before the Senate Appropriations Committee, 87 Cong. 1 sess. (1961).

TABLE 19. Estimated Percentage Shares of Procurement for Selected States and All Regions, 1952, 1956, and 1962

($\beta=.2$ unless otherwise indicated)

State or Region		Percent of Total Procurement		
		1952	1956	1962
California	$\beta=.3$	11.99	18.68	21.27
	$\beta=.2$	11.10	16.98	19.27
	$\beta=.1$	10.20	15.27	17.27
Colorado		.25	.49	1.37
Connecticut		3.80	5.18	4.08
Florida		.42	.79	1.95
Georgia		1.24	1.42	1.41
Illinois		6.32	6.34	4.29
Indiana		4.64	3.10	2.74
Kansas		1.28	2.25	1.53
Maryland		2.04	2.59	1.99
Massachusetts		3.28	3.30	4.52
Michigan	$\beta=.3$	10.66	2.86	3.27
	$\beta=.2$	10.30	3.57	3.93
	$\beta=.1$	9.94	4.27	4.59
Minnesota		1.12	1.01	1.13
Missouri		2.39	2.38	2.15
New Jersey		5.67	5.74	5.18
New York		13.49	11.58	10.45
North Carolina		1.14	1.44	1.35
Ohio		7.55	6.90	5.68
Pennsylvania		6.11	5.81	5.35
Texas		2.88	4.04	3.79
Utah		.10	.17	1.03
Virginia		1.03	.98	1.64
Washington		2.28	2.72	3.20
Wisconsin		2.31	1.52	1.58
New England		8.47	9.66	9.73
Middle Atlantic		25.27	23.13	20.97
East North Central	$\beta=.3$	31.09	20.01	16.31
	$\beta=.2$	31.12	21.42	18.21
	$\beta=.1$	31.15	22.83	20.11
West North Central		6.07	6.69	6.17
South Atlantic		7.65	8.57	10.04
East South Central		2.30	2.59	2.61
West South Central		4.43	5.73	5.36
Mountain		.82	1.72	3.79
Pacific	$\beta=.3$	14.75	21.92	25.13
	$\beta=.2$	13.88	20.10	22.85
	$\beta=.1$	13.00	18.28	20.57

Source: Table A-2.

118

TABLE 20. Breakdown of Changes in Estimated Shares of Procurement for Important States and All Regions, 1952–56

(Changes are in percentage points; β=.2 unless otherwise indicated)

State or Region		Total	From Changes in s[a]	From Changes in d[b]	From Changes in m[c]
			Change in v		
California	β=.3	+ 6.69	+3.99	+2.60	+ .10
	β=.2	+ 5.88	+3.99	+1.73	+ .16
	β=.1	+ 5.07	+3.99	+ .87	+ .21
Colorado		+ .24	+ .20	+ .04	d
Connecticut		+ 1.38	+1.26	+ .18	− .05
Florida		+ .37	+ .31	+ .01	+ .05
Georgia		+ .18	+ .04	+ .13	+ .01
Illinois		+ .02	+ .03	+ .02	− .02
Indiana		− 1.54	−1.31	− .24	+ .02
Kansas		+ .97	+1.04	− .05	− .01
Maryland		+ .55	+ .42	+ .11	+ .02
Massachusetts		+ .02	+ .09	+ .01	− .08
Michigan	β=.3	− 7.80	−5.10	−2.89	+ .20
	β=.2	− 6.73	−5.10	−1.92	+ .29
	β=.1	− 5.67	−5.10	− .96	+ .39
Minnesota		− .11	− .08	− .03	d
Missouri		− .01	+ .08	− .08	− .01
New Jersey		+ .07	+ .10	+ .04	− .08
New York		− 1.91	−1.79	+ .04	− .16
North Carolina		+ .30	+ .27	+ .04	− .01
Ohio		− .65	− .42	− .28	+ .05
Pennsylvania		− .30	− .05	− .06	− .19
Texas		+ 1.16	+ .89	+ .21	+ .07
Utah		+ .07	+ .06	+ .01	d
Virginia		− .05	− .03	− .02	d
Washington		+ .44	+ .23	+ .23	− .02
Wisconsin		− .79	− .62	− .13	− .03
New England		+ 1.19	+1.30	+ .10	− .20
Middle Atlantic		− 2.14	−1.74	+ .02	− .43
East North Central	β=.3	−11.08	−7.43	−3.84	+ .20
	β=.2	− 9.70	−7.43	−2.56	+ .30
	β=.1	− 8.32	−7.43	−1.28	+ .40
West North Central		+ .62	+ .87	− .20	− .04
South Atlantic		+ .92	+ .61	+ .25	+ .05
East South Central		+ .29	+ .16	+ .04	+ .08
West South Central		+ 1.30	+ .97	+ .25	+ .08
Mountain		+ .90	+ .74	+ .13	+ .02
Pacific	β=.3	+ 7.17	+4.16	+2.95	+ .07
	β=.2	+ 6.22	+4.16	+1.96	+ .11
	β=.1	+ 5.28	+4.16	+ .98	+ .14

Source: Calculated from Table A-2.

[a] Equal to α $(s_{1956}-s_{1952})$, where $\alpha=.5$.

[b] Equal to β $(d_{1956}-d_{1952})$, where $\beta=.2$ unless otherwise indicated.

[c] Equal to $(1-\alpha-\beta)$ $(m_{1956}-m_{1952})$.

[d] Less than .005.

119

TABLE 21. Breakdown of Changes in Estimated Shares of Procurement for Important States and All Regions, 1956–62

(Changes are in percentage points; $\beta = .2$ unless otherwise indicated)

State or Region			Change in v		
		Total	From Changes in s^a	From Changes in d^b	From Changes in m^c
California	$\beta=.3$	+2.59	+1.33	+1.11	+ .15
	$\beta=.2$	+2.29	+1.33	+ .74	+ .22
	$\beta=.1$	+2.00	+1.33	+ .37	+ .30
Colorado		+ .88	+ .69	+ .18	+ .02
Connecticut		−1.10	−1.05	− .04	− .02
Florida		+1.16	+ .68	+ .42	+ .06
Georgia		− .01	+ .01	− .08	+ .05
Illinois		−2.05	−1.38	− .60	− .08
Indiana		− .36	− .09	− .33	+ .06
Kansas		− .72	− .62	− .11	d
Maryland		− .60	− .37	− .25	+ .02
Massachusetts		+1.22	+1.02	+ .26	− .06
Michigan	$\beta=.3$	+ .41	+ .70	− .12	− .17
	$\beta=.2$	+ .36	+ .70	− .08	− .25
	$\beta=.1$	+ .32	+ .70	− .04	− .33
Minnesota		+ .12	+ .07	d	+ .06
Missouri		− .23	− .27	+ .02	+ .02
New Jersey		− .56	− .40	− .21	+ .05
New York		−1.13	− .70	− .28	− .15
North Carolina		− .09	− .18	d	+ .09
Ohio		−1.22	− .68	− .31	− .23
Pennsylvania		− .46	− .25	− .02	− .19
Texas		− .25	− .23	− .07	+ .05
Utah		+ .86	+ .68	+ .17	d
Virginia		+ .66	+ .52	+ .09	+ .05
Washington		+ .48	+ .15	+ .34	− .02
Wisconsin		+ .06	+ .03	+ .02	d
New England		+ .07	− .12	+ .30	− .11
Middle Atlantic		−2.16	−1.36	− .51	− .29
East North Central	$\beta=.3$	−3.70	−1.43	−1.95	− .33
	$\beta=.2$	−3.21	−1.43	−1.30	− .49
	$\beta=.1$	−2.72	−1.43	− .64	− .66
West North Central		− .52	− .59	− .04	+ .11
South Atlantic		+1.47	+ .94	+ .21	+ .33
East South Central		+ .02	− .08	− .03	+ .13
West South Central		− .37	− .34	− .11	+ .07
Mountain		+2.07	+1.61	+ .42	+ .05
Pacific	$\beta=.3$	+3.21	+1.48	+1.59	+ .14
	$\beta=.2$	+2.75	+1.48	+1.06	+ .20
	$\beta=.1$	+2.29	+1.48	+ .53	+ .27

Source: Same as for Table 20.
a Equal to α ($s_{1962} - s_{1956}$), where $\alpha = .5$.
b Equal to β ($d_{1962} - d_{1956}$), where $\beta = .2$ unless otherwise indicated.
c Equal to $(1 - \alpha - \beta)$ ($m_{1962} - m_{1956}$).
d Less than .005.

TABLE 22. Breakdown of Changes in Estimated Shares of Procurement for Important States and All Regions, 1952–62

(Changes are in percentage points; $\beta=.2$ unless otherwise indicated)

State or Region		Total	From Changes in s[a]	From Changes in d[b]	From Changes in m[c]
			Change in v		
California	$\beta=.3$	+ 9.28	+5.32	+3.71	+ .26
	$\beta=.2$	+ 8.17	+5.32	+2.47	+ .38
	$\beta=.1$	+ 7.07	+5.32	+1.24	+ .51
Colorado		+ 1.12	+ .89	+ .22	+ .02
Connecticut		+ .28	+ .21	+ .14	− .06
Florida		+ 1.53	+ .98	+ .44	+ .11
Georgia		+ .17	+ .06	+ .05	+ .06
Illinois		− 2.03	−1.35	− .58	− .10
Indiana		− 1.90	−1.40	− .58	+ .08
Kansas		+ .25	+ .41	− .16	− .01
Maryland		− .05	+ .04	− .14	+ .04
Massachusetts		+ 1.24	+1.11	+ .27	− .15
Michigan	$\beta=.3$	− 7.39	−4.41	−3.02	+ .03
	$\beta=.2$	− 6.37	−4.41	−2.01	+ .04
	$\beta=.1$	− 5.35	−4.41	−1.01	+ .06
Minnesota		+ .01	− .01	− .03	+ .05
Missouri		− .24	− .19	− .07	+ .01
New Jersey		− .49	− .30	− .17	− .03
New York		− 3.04	−2.49	− .24	− .32
North Carolina		+ .21	+ .09	+ .03	+ .09
Ohio		− 1.87	−1.10	− .58	− .18
Pennsylvania		− .76	− .31	− .08	− .38
Texas		+ .91	+ .65	+ .14	+ .12
Utah		+ .93	+ .73	+ .18	+ .01
Virginia		+ .61	+ .49	+ .07	+ .05
Washington		+ .92	+ .39	+ .57	− .04
Wisconsin		− .73	− .59	− .11	− .03
New England		+ 1.26	+1.18	+ .41	− .32
Middle Atlantic		− 4.30	−3.09	− .50	− .72
East North Central	$\beta=.3$	−14.78	−8.85	−5.79	− .13
	$\beta=.2$	−12.91	−8.85	−3.86	− .20
	$\beta=.1$	−11.04	−8.85	−1.93	− .26
West North Central		+ .10	+ .29	− .25	+ .07
South Atlantic		+ 2.39	+1.56	+ .44	+ .38
East South Central		+ .31	+ .08	+ .01	+ .21
West South Central		+ .93	+ .62	+ .15	+ .15
Mountain		+ 2.97	+2.34	+ .56	+ .06
Pacific	$\beta=.3$	+10.38	+5.64	+4.54	+ .21
	$\beta=.2$	+ 8.97	+5.64	+3.03	+ .31
	$\beta=.1$	+ 7.57	+5.64	+1.51	+ .41

Source: Same as for Table 20.
[a] Equal to α ($s_{1962} - s_{1952}$), where $\alpha = .5$.
[b] Equal to β ($d_{1962} - d_{1952}$), where $\beta = .2$ unless otherwise indicated.
[c] Equal to $(1 - \alpha - \beta)$ ($m_{1962} - m_{1952}$).
[d] Less than .005.

between California and New York gradually increased after 1954, regardless of which of the three values of β is used in measuring the gap.[6]

New York's share actually rose somewhat in 1954, but then fell gradually in 1955 and 1956, after which it remained stable until it fell somewhat in 1961 and 1962. While suffering from the cutback in ordnance and production equipment, New York received large contracts for aircraft, ships, and electronics.

The East North Central Region also suffered greatly in the post-Korean cutback. Its aircraft and electronics manufacturing were not great enough to maintain its share. Declines were greatest in Michigan, which depended most on vehicles. In 1952, Michigan received nearly 14 percent of prime contracts (not adjusted by moving average); in 1954 its share was negative due to cancellations, and by 1962 it had only risen to just over 2.5 percent.

Some states whose share during the Korean period was relatively insignificant achieved a comparatively high, sustained growth rate in the later 1950's. Florida is an outstanding example; from less than 0.5 percent of procurement purchases during the Korean period, its share rose to about 2 percent in 1962. Much of this was due to the building and expansion of the Cape Kennedy complex, which required construction, services, and miscellaneous contracts, but missile manufacturing also contributed to the growth rate.

Colorado's share increased more than five times between 1952 and 1962, primarily because of the emergence of the Martin-Marietta Company as a large missile contractor in Denver during the period. Also in the Mountain Region, Arizona and Utah greatly increased their shares, with missile, propulsion, and electronics contracts leading the accelerated growth.

[6] Even with as high a weight for defense-related industries as .3, the 1959 and 1960 estimates of v for California fall short of its share of prime contracts, unadjusted for timing, by 1.99 and 2.63 percentage points, respectively. They fall short of the contract shares adjusted for timing by 2.09 and 2.18 percentage points, respectively, in the two years. These results contrast with those of George A. Steiner, who estimated total defense procurement in *southern* California in fiscal year 1960. Steiner assumed, and termed his assumption a "conservative" one, that the defense subcontracts and purchase orders flowing into southern California from contractors in other states at least matched the leakages from subcontracts and purchases made outside the area by its own prime contractors. See Committee for Economic Development, Southern California Associates, *National Defense and Southern California, 1961-1970* (The Associates, 1961).

Tables 20, 21, and 22 show that changes in contract shares contributed most to changes in estimated shares of procurement. If the estimation procedures are accepted, therefore, changes in the distribution of prime contracts seem to be rather good indicators of changes in the distribution of purchases on a value-added basis. At any rate, it is extremely unlikely that changes in a state's share of prime contracts will be offset enough by changes in the other distributions to maintain the former share of procurement.

Factors in Changes of Relative Shares

The primary cause of the great change in the regional distribution of procurement was the drastic change in the composition of military items purchased. Table 23 summarizes the shifts in weapons which took place after the Korean War. It should be noted that, low as the fiscal year 1962 amount for the "Tank-Automotive . . ." programs was, it was rather lower (12.4 percent) in the fiscal year 1961, before emphasis on conventional warfare was renewed.

The distribution by state and region of prime contracts in the Korean period was quite similar to that in World War II (the only significant changes were a decline for the East North Central Region and a rise for the Pacific, but both changes were smaller than

TABLE 23. Changes in the Composition of Military Hard Goods Purchases, 1942–44, 1953, and 1962

| Item | Percent of Value of Deliveries | Percent of Value of Deliveries | Percent of Value of Contracts, FY 1962 |
	World War II, FY's 1942–44	FY 1953	
Aircraft	27.3	31.5	25.7
Missiles	0	.5	33.7
Ships	26.2	6.8	7.4
Electronics	6.6	11.2	16.6
Tank-Automotive, Weapons, Ammunition, Production Equipment and Miscellaneous	39.9	50.0	16.5

Source: U. S. Department of Defense, *The Changing Patterns of Defense Procurement*, and *Military Prime Contract Awards and Subcontract Payments* (June 1963).

ones in the same direction between the Korean period and 1962).[7]
The bill of goods for the Korean conflict still resembled that of
World War II, but changes in defense technology transformed military requirements after the Korean period. The decline in the importance of vehicles, ordnance, and production equipment was
bound to have a depressing effect upon those states which were
heavily dependent upon their capacity in these lines for defense orders. At the same time, the dramatic rise in importance of missiles
beneficially affected regions suited to their manufacture.

The distribution of research and development contracts is likely
to be a significant determinant of the distribution of production
contracts in the future. This is true both for firms and for areas.[8]
Defense research and development in recent years has been relatively
less important in the North Central Region than in the country
as a whole. Aircraft, vehicles, and ordnance contracts are
significant there, but in these programs, research and development
has been less important than in other programs.

Nonprofit institutions in the Midwest have been less successful
in gaining research contracts than have those located in the eastern
coastal strip from Boston to Washington, and those in certain areas
of California; the Midwest's share of such awards is not commensu-
rate with its shares of university resources and higher degrees
granted.[9] Although these research contracts are quantitatively not
very important, they have long-range significance and may
influence industrial location decisions made by actual or potential
prime contractors. Their importance has been debated, however;
some feel that the character of a university is shaped by the needs
of firms in that university's area, not that firms are attracted by the
quality of universities.[10] In fact, there is probably something of a

[7] U. S. Department of Defense, *The Changing Patterns of Defense Procurement,*
passim.

[8] *Ibid.,* pp. 7-8.

[9] *Ibid.,* p. 10. These contracts let to institutions are extremely concentrated.
In fiscal year 1964, just over half the value went to Massachusetts and Cali-
fornia; the addition of Maryland and New York accounts for nearly 70 percent.
See U. S. Department of Defense, *Military Prime Contract Awards by Region and
State, Fiscal Years 1962, 1963, and 1964,* pp. 69-71.

[10] I am indebted to Henry Glass for this line of thought. Civilian space activities in the gulf coast area are stimulating course improvement and expansion
and research in the sciences by regional educational institutions; see "Space Age

"vicious circle" operating here in areas which in the past, for some reason, have not been successful in attracting contracts.

Company Policies and Regional Patterns

Some persons may explain the Midwest's decline as follows: "Companies there did not want defense business except during the all-out needs of World War II and Korea; they preferred to stick to civilian markets." Such an explanation need not be uncharitable. After Korea, civilian demand appeared strong enough to absorb full efforts of companies in traditional consumer or producer goods output. Such firms may have felt little need to keep up with rapidly changing defense needs.[11]

For some companies, however, adjustment to new defense technology was a matter of existence. Especially after Korea, with a forecast decline in long production runs of aircraft, aircraft firms were forced into work on missiles and other newer weapons. Their civilian markets alone were hopelessly inadequate to sustain operations. As the economy's growth slackened, other firms realized the importance of defense business, but their efforts to regain a place in procurement were made difficult because aircraft manufacturers and specialized firms had entrenched themselves.

For familiar reasons—a mild climate, widely available space, a cumulative process of improvements in external economies and growth in a skilled labor supply, and some unique circumstances in some localities[12]—the aircraft industry was concentrated in southern California and in a few other states even before World War II. (The war saw decentralization via expansion in other regions, but afterward the older core remained the major center; in the Korean period dispersion was not great.) On the other hand, the Midwest and parts of the Middle Atlantic states were traditional bases of companies that returned to civilian production.

Boom is Bringing a Revolution to the Southwest," *New York Times*, August 25, 1963, p. 56.

[11] For some comments along this line, see the statement by Ron M. Linton, in *Impact of Defense Spending on Labor Surplus Areas, 1962*, Hearing before the Senate Select Committee on Small Business, 87 Cong. 2 sess. (1962), p. 59.

[12] William Glenn Cunningham, *The Aircraft Industry: A Study in Industrial Location* (L. L. Morrison, 1951), *passim*.

The role of *companies* is of course important. Their location decisions are crucial for regions, and, as noted above, many states receive most of their contracts because of the presence of one or two contractors.

CHAPTER VIII

The Regional Distribution of Payrolls

THE STATE DISTRIBUTION of military payrolls for selected years is shown in Table 24, and Department of Defense civilian wages and salaries in Table 25. (Data for all years of the period 1947-62 are given in the General Appendix.) For civilian wages, the year 1952 was chosen as representative of the Korean period. For military wages, the dollar amounts given are those for 1952, but the percentages are calculated for the entire period 1951-53, since there were rapid shifts of forces during that period which might distort states' shares.

The military payroll figures are the official estimates of the Office of Business Economics prepared in the fashion outlined in the appendix to Chapter V; note especially that states' shares in *population* are given some weight to reflect dependents' allotments.

Geographical Concentration of Payrolls

Table 26 presents typical concentration measures, which show that both kinds of payrolls were less concentrated than procurement

127

TABLE 24. Military Payrolls, by State and Region, Selected Years

(Amounts in millions of dollars)

State or Region	1947 Amount	1947 Percent	1952 Amount	1951–1953 Percent	1956 Amount	1956 Percent	1962 Amount	1962 Percent
Maine	8	.28	33	.42	56	.72	73	.83
New Hampshire	9	.31	16	.19	23	.29	42	.48
Vermont	2	.07	7	.08	7	.09	5	.06
Massachusetts	66	2.28	212	2.57	184	2.36	210	2.38
Connecticut	20	.69	44	.55	48	.62	63	.71
Rhode Island	39	1.34	99	1.19	105	1.35	102	1.16
New England	144	4.96	410	5.00	424	5.44	495	5.61
New York	152	5.24	334	3.96	318	4.08	311	3.52
New Jersey	130	4.48	246	2.94	182	2.33	244	2.77
Pennsylvania	94	3.24	212	2.44	164	2.10	158	1.79
Middle Atlantic	376	12.96	792	9.33	664	8.51	713	8.08
Ohio	61	2.10	145	1.71	145	1.86	161	1.82
Indiana	23	.79	98	1.29	57	.73	72	.82
Illinois	116	4.00	273	3.22	268	3.44	275	3.12
Michigan	47	1.62	121	1.38	101	1.29	147	1.67
Wisconsin	15	.52	66	.75	43	.55	48	.54
East North Central	262	9.03	702	8.35	613	7.86	703	7.97
Minnesota	13	.45	38	.46	42	.54	47	.53
Iowa	13	.45	26	.31	27	.35	26	.29
Missouri	26	.90	127	1.60	129	1.66	148	1.68
North Dakota	2	.07	7	.09	7	.09	41	.46
South Dakota	6	.21	27	.32	26	.33	26	.29
Nebraska	12	.41	31	.37	53	.68	85	.96
Kansas	32	1.10	116	1.48	147	1.88	168	1.90
West North Central	104	3.58	372	4.63	431	5.52	542	6.14
Kentucky	56	1.93	233	2.86	149	1.91	215	2.44
Tennessee	32	1.10	94	1.12	92	1.18	101	1.14
Alabama	40	1.38	143	1.78	116	1.49	125	1.42
Mississippi	32	1.10	87	1.11	83	1.06	125	1.42
East South Central	160	5.52	557	6.86	440	5.64	566	6.42

Arkansas	17	.59	65	.81	78	1.00	81	.92
Oklahoma	32	1.10	126	1.47	123	1.58	151	1.71
Louisiana	35	1.21	154	1.83	138	1.77	163	1.85
Texas	193	6.65	737	8.92	705	9.04	773	8.76
West South Central	277	9.55	1,082	13.02	1,044	13.38	1,168	13.24
Delaware	2	.07	13	.17	29	.37	35	.40
Maryland	94	3.24	312	3.63	292	3.74	267	3.03
District of Columbia	53	1.83	79	.96	80	1.03	82	.93
Virginia	269	9.27	668	8.08	548	7.03	539	6.11
West Virginia	11	.38	18	.21	17	.22	15	.17
North Carolina	104	3.58	280	3.50	269	3.45	351	3.98
South Carolina	66	2.28	215	2.62	186	2.38	223	2.53
Georgia	71	2.45	282	3.37	269	3.45	343	3.89
Florida	136	4.69	306	3.66	347	4.45	367	4.16
South Atlantic	806	27.78	2,173	26.20	2,037	26.11	2,222	25.18
Montana	5	.17	19	.23	22	.28	39	.44
Idaho	2	.07	23	.22	18	.23	28	.32
Wyoming	7	.24	32	.37	37	.47	17	.19
Colorado	41	1.41	116	1.41	148	1.90	163	1.85
Utah	7	.24	18	.23	19	.24	24	.27
Nevada	1	.03	19	.24	28	.36	35	.40
Arizona	18	.62	70	.79	85	1.09	86	.97
New Mexico	20	.69	87	1.04	87	1.12	95	1.08
Mountain	101	3.48	384	4.54	444	5.69	487	5.52
Washington	113	3.90	236	2.99	236	3.03	273	3.09
Oregon	12	.41	31	.37	27	.35	34	.39
California	464	15.99	1,325	15.50	1,130	14.49	1,309	14.84
Pacific	589	20.30	1,592	18.86	1,393	17.86	1,616	18.32
Hawaii	80	2.76	125	1.51	165	2.12	192	2.18
Alaska	n.a.	n.a.	137	1.70	143	1.83	121	1.37
United States	2,901	100.00	8,326	100.00	7,800	100.00	8,823	100.00

Source: Table A-3.
n.a. Not available.

129

TABLE 25. Department of Defense Civilian Wages and Salaries, by State and Region, Selected Years

(Amounts in millions of dollars)

State or Region	1947		1952		1956		1962	
	Amount	Percent	Amount	Percent	Amount	Percent	Amount	Percent
Maine	9	.44	23	.49	21	.43	36	.57
New Hampshire	9	.44	24	.52	20	.41	36	.57
Vermont	a	.01	1	.02	1	.02	1	.02
Massachusetts	51	2.48	157	3.37	140	2.88	182	2.88
Connecticut	4	.19	8	.17	12	.25	18	.29
Rhode Island	20	.97	35	.75	41	.84	50	.79
New England	93	4.51	248	5.33	235	4.84	324	5.13
New York	145	7.04	342	7.34	311	6.40	327	5.18
New Jersey	57	2.77	141	3.03	151	3.11	200	3.17
Pennsylvania	159	7.72	344	7.39	335	6.90	449	7.11
Middle Atlantic	361	17.52	827	17.76	797	16.41	976	15.46
Ohio	91	4.42	226	4.85	233	4.80	259	4.10
Indiana	22	1.07	81	1.74	67	1.38	75	1.19
Illinois	60	2.91	175	3.76	141	2.90	173	2.74
Michigan	15	.73	65	1.40	51	1.05	91	1.44
Wisconsin	3	.15	9	.19	10	.21	14	.22
East North Central	191	9.27	556	11.94	502	10.34	612	9.69
Minnesota	4	.19	6	.13	8	.16	13	.21
Iowa	2	.10	4	.09	17	.35	24	.38
Missouri	45	2.18	42	.90	63	1.30	85	1.35
North Dakota	1	.05	4	.09	3	.06	7	.11
South Dakota	3	.15	7	.15	8	.16	12	.19
Nebraska	12	.58	26	.56	25	.51	27	.43
Kansas	13	.63	27	.58	37	.76	34	.54
West North Central	80	3.88	116	2.49	161	3.31	202	3.20
Kentucky	21	1.02	57	1.22	53	1.09	68	1.08
Tennessee	22	1.07	39	.84	47	.97	48	.76
Alabama	38	1.84	113	2.43	157	3.23	220	3.48
Mississippi	17	.83	24	.52	31	.64	38	.60
East South Central	98	4.76	233	5.00	288	5.93	374	5.92

	Value	%	Value	%	Value	%	Value	%
Arkansas	8	.39	19	.41	25	.51	30	.48
Oklahoma	43	2.09	111	2.38	120	2.47	149	2.36
Louisiana	24	1.17	36	.77	39	.80	44	.70
Texas	111	5.39	258	5.54	301	6.20	359	5.68
West South Central	186	9.03	424	9.10	485	9.99	582	9.22
Delaware	a	.01	2	.04	7	.14	8	.13
Maryland	92	4.47	199	4.27	243	5.00	367	5.81
District of Columbia	99	4.81	195	4.19	194	3.99	168	2.66
Virginia	163	7.91	337	7.24	369	7.60	531	8.41
West Virginia	4	.19	8	.17	6	.12	6	.10
North Carolina	25	1.21	37	.79	43	.89	59	.93
South Carolina	31	1.50	57	1.22	63	1.30	92	1.46
Georgia	50	2.43	127	2.73	140	2.88	184	2.91
Florida	58	2.82	94	2.02	127	2.61	155	2.45
South Atlantic	522	25.34	1,056	22.68	1,192	24.54	1,570	24.86
Montana	2	.10	3	.06	4	.08	8	.13
Idaho	3	.15	5	.11	4	.08	3	.05
Wyoming	2	.10	5	.11	7	.14	4	.06
Colorado	16	.78	65	1.40	69	1.42	89	1.41
Utah	32	1.55	98	2.10	87	1.79	119	1.88
Nevada	4	.19	11	.24	15	.31	16	.25
Arizona	8	.39	20	.43	33	.68	48	.76
New Mexico	8	.39	22	.47	42	.86	61	.97
Mountain	75	3.64	229	4.92	261	5.37	348	5.51
Washington	80	3.88	202	4.34	163	3.36	157	2.49
Oregon	10	.49	25	.54	20	.41	23	.36
California	362	17.57	740	15.89	751	15.46	975	15.44
Pacific	452	21.94	967	20.76	934	19.23	1,155	18.29
Hawaii	n.a.	n.a.	n.a.	n.a.	n.a.	n.a.	123	1.95
Alaska	n.a.	n.a.	n.a.	n.a.	n.a.	n.a.	49	.78
United States	2,060	100.00	4,657	100.00	4,857	100.00	6,315	100.00

Source: Table A-4.
n.a. Not available.
a Less than $.5 million.

131

**TABLE 26. Concentration of Military and Civilian Wages,
Selected Years**

Percent in:	Military Wages			
	1947	1951–53 Total	1956	1962
Top Four States	37.4	36.5	35.0	33.9
	(Calif., Va., Texas, N.Y.)	(Calif., Texas, Va., N.Y.)	(Calif., Texas, Va., Florida)	(Calif., Texas, Va., Florida)
Top Eight States	54.4	50.6	49.7	48.4
	(Fla., N.J., Ill., Wash.)	(Fla., Md., N.C., Ga.)	(N.Y., Md., N.C., Ga.)	(N.C., Ga., N.Y., Ill.)
Top Fifteen States	74.3	70.2	67.5	66.8
Bottom Ten States	1.8	2.0	2.5	2.8

Percent in:	Civilian Wages			
	1947	1952	1956	1962
Top Four States	40.2	37.9	36.4	36.8
	(Calif. Va., Pa., N.Y.)	(Calif., Pa., N.Y., Va.)	(Calif., Va., Pa., N.Y.)	(Calif., Va., Pa., Md.)
Top Eight States	58.3	56.9	56.4	55.2
	(Texas, D.C., Md., Ohio)	(Texas, Ohio, Wash., Md.)	(Texas, Md., Ohio, D.C.)	(Texas, N.Y., Ohio, Alab.)
Top Fifteen States	77.8	78.8	77.3	74.5
Bottom Ten States	1.0	1.1	1.2	1.2

Source: Calculated from Tables A-3 and A-4.

purchases shown in Table 18. There were slight decreases in concentration between 1952 and 1962, and somewhat greater decreases between 1947 and 1962, especially in military payrolls.

Aspects of the Regional Distribution

Some of the factors determining the geographical location of military and civilian personnel are obvious. The Washington, D.C., area is an important headquarters location. Terrain, climate, and space are important reasons for the location of air bases and Army training centers in the southern, plains, and mountain areas of the country. Coastal locations are necessary for many naval installations, and strategic locations account for other concentrations of personnel. Some civilian wages are paid in "in-house" research and development and manufacturing facilities, the location of which is often explicable by ordinary industrial location theory. Large states in the East North Central and Middle Atlantic Regions not only have large populations, but also numerous support installations such as quartermaster depots and distribution and warehousing facilities. Ohio benefits from the location there of a large complex which supports aeronautical research and procurement.

Some states have very small shares of military payrolls because they have small populations and few installations. It should be noted, however, that a number of states with very small shares of procurement have larger shares of military wages; examples are the District of Columbia, the Dakotas, Alaska, Hawaii, and several states in the South and the Mountain Region. These states have relatively little industrial capacity, especially in defense-related industries, but have special advantages for training centers and other military bases.

Occupations of civilian employees of the military establishment are extremely varied. Many clerical and office support workers are required at installations and headquarters; scientists, engineers, mathematicians, attorneys, auditors and other professionals are numerous; less skilled workers such as mechanics and blue-collar personnel are also important. All three services conduct in-house research and development and manufacturing, notably in arsenals, shipyards, and printing plants; aircraft maintenance and repair depots also utilize civilian personnel. The Defense Supply Agency employs civilians in purchasing, storing, and distributing supplies. Department of Defense personnel supervise operations at contractors' plants and they administer procurement. In-house research and development may be conducted in close cooperation with contractors or in geographical areas with concentrations of certain industries, thus civilian employment may be significant in important procurement localities for this reason as well.

Some amount of summary information is available on location of the services' own industrial activity. This is helpful in explaining trends in civilian employment discussed below. Tables 27 and 28 give information on manufacturing plants owned and operated by the Department of Defense, for 1954 and 1958. Table 28 shows that almost all such manufacturing is of ordnance and ships, and it shows a substantial decline in ordnance. If information were available for the Korean years, when ordnance needs were high, a more

TABLE 27. Employees and Value Added for Department of Defense Manufacturing Establishments, by State and Region, 1954 and 1958[a]

(Dollar amounts in millions)

State or Region	1954		1958		
	Employees	Value Added	Employees	Payroll	Value Added
New Hampshire	7,907	$ 35	7,390	$ 41	$ 42
Massachusetts	18,376	91	12,635	72	84
New England	26,283	127	20,025	113	126
New York	19,396	113	15,040	87	101
New Jersey	3,839	16	1,915	11	19
Pennsylvania	18,919	97	14,297	74	79
Middle Atlantic	42,154	226	31,252	171	199
Indiana	3,863	24	185	1	2
Illinois	8,746	47	4,034	23	30
East North Central	12,642	71	4 219	24	32
West North Central	2,653	12	—	—	—
Maryland	3,366	14	1,263	6	8
District of Columbia	8,732	53	5,266	29	30
Virginia	13,474	63	11,880	65	69
South Carolina	6,344	32	7,075	37	37
Georgia	2,056	9	702	3	3
Florida	—	—	369	2	4
South Atlantic	33,972	171	26,555	144	152
Kentucky	1,474	9	1,737	10	10
Alabama	1,063	6	5,455	42	43
East South Central	2,537	15	7,192	52	53
West South Central	5,874	31	844	4	5
Mountain	2,747	16	1,251	7	7
Washington	14,616	80	10,942	64	74
California	29,406	171	23,160	139	151
Pacific	44,022	251	34,102	203	225
United States	172,844	920	125,440	717	799

Source: U. S. Bureau of the Census, *U. S. Census of Manufactures: 1958*, Vol. 1 (1963), p. SR-1.

[a] The United States totals exclude Alaska and Hawaii. All figures exclude establishments serving only a single base or port, such as bakeries and machine shops. No military personnel are included in the employment and payroll data. For shipyards, the value added is based on deductions from a base figure of new construction and repair performed, not shipped.

TABLE 28. Employees and Value Added for Department of Defense Manufacturing Establishments, by Industry, 1954 and 1958[a]

(Dollar amounts in millions)

SIC Code	1954		1958		
	Employees	Value Added	Employees	Payroll	Value Added
2311, Men's Clothes	2,429	$ 9	2,153	$ 10	$ 11
3662, Electronics	—	—	1,915	11	19
3731, 3732, Ships and Boats	109,754	580	91,083	523	571
1900, Ordnance	56,884	312	29,826	174	198
All Other	3,817	18	103	1	1
United States total	172,884	920	125,440	717	799

Source: *U. S. Bureau of the Census, U. S. Census of Manufactures: 1958,* Vol. 1 (1963), p. SR-1.
[a] The United States totals exclude Alaska and Hawaii. All figures exclude establishments serving only a single base or port, such as bakeries and machine shops. No military personnel are included in the employment and payroll data. For shipyards, the value added is based on deductions from a base figure of new construction and repair performed, not shipped.

pronounced decline would undoubtedly be evident. A comparison of Table 27 with Table A-4 will make clear how important industrial wages are in some states.

Although not shown in Tables 27 and 28, it is known that the in-house ordnance activity has been important in the traditional manufacturing centers of New England, and in the Middle Atlantic and East North Central states, where arsenals were long ago established. Not only has the volume of work declined at these arsenals, but some have been closed and sold.

The location of shipbuilding, now the largest industrial activity, is easily explained by the need for sites near water and for easy access to materials. As of early 1965, the Navy had eleven yards, with a total employment of about 80,000 men.[1] World War II peak

[1] Most of this and the next paragraph is based on: *Utilization of Naval Shipyard Facilities,* Hearing before the House Committee on Armed Services, 87 Cong. 1 sess. (1961), *passim; January 1961 Economic Report of the President and Economic Situation and Outlook,* Hearing before the Joint Economic Committee, 87 Cong. 1 sess. (1961), statement of Charles J. Hitch, pp. 621-22, and 640-44; *Department of Defense Appropriations for 1963,* Hearing before the House Committee on Appropriations, 87 Cong. 2 sess. (1962), Pt. 3, pp. 281-82, and Pt. 4, pp. 284 ff.; *Department of Defense Appropriations for 1965,* Hearing before the Senate Committee on Appropriations, 88 Cong. 2 sess. (1964), Pt. 2, p. 588; *Department of Defense Appropriations for 1966,* Hearing before the House Committee on Appropriations, 89 Cong. 1 sess. (1965), Pt. 4, p. 300.

employment was 353,000 and the Korean war peak was 140,000 in 1952. The Navy yards account for much of the civilian employment of the defense establishment in certain states. New Hampshire, Massachusetts, New York, Pennsylvania, Virginia, South Carolina, California, Washington, and Hawaii are the nine states where the yards are located.

The Navy has continued operation of its shipyards despite evidence that they generate higher costs than do private yards. Public law now requires that some new construction be done in Navy yards, and in fact, that every other combat vessel be built there unless the alternation is changed by the President in the public interest. The smaller Navy yards have been maintained by giving them most of the conversion, alteration, and repair work; while over 80 percent of new construction has been going to private yards, only 35 percent of other work has (fiscal years 1963-64). The Navy has desired to retain its own facilities in order to maintain a reserve of capacity, to insure integration with fleet movements, and to insure work being done in case of strikes at private yards or refusal of private yards to do emergency work in great haste.

There has long been dispute between the Navy and the private shipbuilding industry on the allocation of work between Navy yards and privately-owned yards. Public awareness of this controversy has been recently heightened by the announcement of plans of the Defense Department to close some Navy yards.

General abandonment of the Navy yards would bring obvious changes in the distribution of total spending. Some states—Louisiana, Mississippi, Florida, and Maryland—have only private yards or predominately private yards. The reverse is true in South Carolina. Other states have considerable capacity in both public and private yards.

Regional Changes in Military Payrolls

The rapid increase in active-duty forces brought substantial changes in regional distribution in the Korean period, as compared with that for 1947. Most states with training centers increased their shares of the national total. The slower growth in headquarters and Navy personnel had an effect on some states. Areas such as the Middle Atlantic and East North Central Regions, whose large shares depended upon large populations or upon support personnel more than upon training centers, suffered relative declines.

After Korea, certain states with Air Force training centers and other large air bases benefitted from increasing emphasis on air and missile warfare. Air Force strength increased relative to that of the other two services after the post-Korean cutback. Expansion of bases to suit new aircraft, conversion of some to ICBM bases, and construction of new missile bases all favored the Southwest, Mountain, and Pacific Regions.[2] Some states in these areas also increased both their shares of procurement and their shares of military payrolls. Kansas, Nebraska, Oklahoma, Montana, Idaho, and Nevada all increased shares in payrolls in the later 1950's. In some cases, an upward trend in the first post-Korean years was later reversed. Considering the nature of the payroll estimates, relative gains in population also contributed to rising shares in payrolls.

Losses in Maryland, the District of Columbia, and Virginia brought the South Atlantic Region's share down after 1956. The Middle Atlantic Region's relative losses after Korea were not as great as they had been between 1947 and the earlier 1950's, and the three states in the region showed greatly different movements. The East North Central Region's percentage in 1962 was close to that of the Korean period and not far below that of 1947, except for Indiana, which suffered a large net decline.

The state distribution of military forces and payrolls is difficult to explain in detail, and many trends and sharp movements are puzzling. After 1956, the relative strengths of the three military services changed little. The total number of active-duty personnel declined steadily from 1952 to the middle of 1961; the subsequent rise, although relatively greater in the Army, is not sufficient to explain some changes in regional shares. The scanty literature on all of this concentrates on short-term movements.[3] The many single decisions

[2] ICBM bases have been located in outlying areas such as the plains and mountain states for a number of reasons, including limitations on missile range. Security from coastal attack (of course, *defensive* missile bases are located near coasts), terrain, dispersal, and availability of government-owned land are other factors. But since installation time is affected by climate and costs by proximity to existing communities, and since range has increased, bases have also been set up in California, Texas, Arizona, and Arkansas. See *Military Construction Authorization, Fiscal Year 1959,* Hearing before the Senate Committee on Armed Services, 85 Cong. 2 sess. (1958), pp. 326 ff.

[3] For example, the annual articles on personal income by state (variously titled), in the August issues of the *Survey of Current Business.*

about deployment and training which produced the results now available have not been summarized or explained in any general way. However, four broad trends can be assumed to be important: the new emphasis on air and missile warfare; the sharp rise and subsequent cutback (until 1961) in conventional forces during the Korean and post-Korean period; the rapid growth of procurement in some states; and differences among states in population growth, and thus presumably in their representation in the armed forces. These factors, if considered together with the particular suitability of certain areas for installations—due to natural features or to historical accident—help explain regional changes.

Regional Changes in Civilian Wages

The literature is even less adequate on the question of changes in civilian wages. Defense wages are usually lumped with all federal government civilian wages in discussions of regional wage patterns. It is apparent, however, that changes in civilian wages have differed from those which affected military payrolls.

First, changes in civilian wages between 1947 and 1952 were generally not as great as those in military payrolls, and some were in opposite directions to changes in military payrolls. Only the Mountain and South Atlantic Regions saw significant relative movements in the same direction as in military wages. The share of the East North Central Region rose, partly from increases in ordnance manufacturing and partly from needs for employees to administer procurement operations.

Between the end of the Korean War and 1962, relative declines were suffered by the Middle Atlantic and East North Central states. Declines in procurement and in in-house ordnance and shipbuilding played some part. In addition, more and more of the total cost of ships was spent outside of shipyards, for electronics and propulsion. Thus shipyard employment could fall even as naval forces were maintained and strengthened.

A few large relative shares stand out in other states. Large gains were registered by Maryland and New Mexico for the whole 1952-62 period, and large losses by the District of Columbia and the state of Washington. Many states showed movement in one direction between 1952 and 1956, and in just the opposite direction between 1956 and 1962.

As stated above, little has been written on the distribution of civilian payrolls. Their importance for regional development has not been treated in a way which reveals the basic causes of shifts. In-house industrial wages are not large enough to be more than a partial cause of changes. Change in the distribution of procurement itself is also relevant, but the connection needs fuller treatment and detailed verification. In-house research and development has undoubtedly been significant in recent years; its regional distribution is perhaps explained by the same factors which have created new centers for military personnel and procurement.

CHAPTER IX

Defense Purchases Policy

THERE IS DISAGREEMENT in the United States on the proper criteria for regional distribution of defense purchases. The official Defense Department policy, in general, is that "the most for the least money" is the only relevant guide, and the actual regional distribution has been defended on cost and performance grounds. Economists generally support least cost as the guide to contract placement, with a frequent proviso that general fiscal and area redevelopment policy, not defense purchasing specifically, should insure full employment in the economy as a whole and alleviate pockets of structural unemployment. I agree with this general position. A majority of Congress has agreed that no extra cost should be paid merely to relieve economic dislocation, although it has allowed extra costs to boost small business. But many officials at the state and local level, and some congressmen as well, have insisted that there ought to be a "fair share" for every firm or geographical area capable of doing the job, or of developing the ability to do so. While he did not proclaim such a "fair share," then-Senator Hubert Humphrey remarked in 1962 that one can give nearly any area a capability if some defense money is pumped in, and that strong research and development areas developed their capabilities through the infusion of Federal money:

I realize it is difficult to get prime contracts in a distressed area, particularly if you have a policy that says: 'Well, there is nobody there to take care of it.' There was nobody out in California to take care of it at first, either. They put them there . . . Any time the Defense Department wants to make a going community, they will do it.[1]

As for cost, social costs can be different from private costs or different again from money costs to the armed services. Even considering only money costs, Senator Humphrey also argued that the Defense Department is not the whole federal government, and he predicted the government would experience lower total costs if contracts were channeled into labor-surplus areas, as a result of lower unemployment insurance and relief costs and of gains in taxes on earned incomes.[2]

An important plea for a "fair share" criterion came with the introduction of Senate Bill 1875 in the 1959 session. Sponsored by Senators Javits and Keating of New York and Case of New Jersey, it was also introduced in the House by every member from the state of New York. Titled the "Armed Services Competitive Procurement Act of 1959," it sought to amend the United States Code to record a declaration of policy by Congress that:

. . . the security of the Nation requires that its economy, and the economy of each section of the country, be maintained at a level which can support its programs for defense and sustain the private economic system, and that procurements by agencies under this chapter have a meaningful effect upon the Nation's economic health. Accordingly, it is the further policy of the Congress that, insofar as is consistent with national security, the needs of the agency, and the character of the products and services being procured—

(i) a fair proportion of purchases made under this chapter be placed with small business concerns; (ii) a fair proportion of purchases made under this chapter be placed with concerns located in areas of substantial labor surplus; and

(iii) in placing purchases under this chapter the procuring agency shall consider the strategic and economic desirability of allocating purchases to different geographical areas of the Nation and to eligible suppliers from whom relatively small proportions of procurement have been purchased. . . .

[1] *Impact of Defense Spending on Labor Surplus Areas, 1962,* Hearing before the Senate Select Committee on Small Business, 87 Cong. 2 sess. (1962), pp. 6-7, 10.

[2] *Ibid.,* p. 55.

Whenever formal advertising is required under section 2304 . . . specifications and invitations for bids shall permit such free and full competition as is consistent with the procurement of the property and services needed by the agency concerned: *Provided,* That invitations to bid in any purchase to be made by formal advertising may be restricted to qualified small business concerns *or concerns in a specified area of the Nation,* unless the head of the agency determines that such restriction would not be consistent with the national interest [emphasis supplied].[3]

What was novel in the bill was the proposed declaration of policy and the setting aside of orders so that proportions of purchases could be made in specific parts of the country, whether with substantial labor surplus or not. The provisions for areas and suppliers "from whom relatively small proportions of procurement have been purchased" seemed to aim at insuring "balance" in the regional impact of procurement. While the language is typically vague and allows any procuring agency discretion and exceptions to a balanced procurement policy, enactment of S. 1875, which did not pass, would certainly have marked a major change in the procurement policies laid down by Congress.

In regard to the proposal, Senator Javits remarked on a shift of defense dollars from New York to California in particular, and noted that the average New Yorker contributed far more in taxes which paid for procurement than did the average Californian, yet received far fewer prime contracts. He expressed the belief that the bill would give states an equal opportunity to compete for contracts currently awarded by negotiation, and that New York and other eastern states would "gradually regain on the merits some of the billions of dollars in defense work presently being so heavily allotted to west coast firms."[4]

When the national economy is running at a low unemployment level, and defense production must compete with and replace other production, it is obvious that the average New Yorker, for example, is best off if the defense dollar is spent under the least cost principle. That is how his tax dollar buys the most defense protection. If production in California is more efficient than in New York, the average

[3] *Military Procurement,* Hearing before the Senate Committee on Armed Services, 86 Cong. 1 sess. (1959), pp. 22-23.

[4] Quoted in *ibid.,* pp. 25-26.

New Yorker is better off if the contracts are placed in California. The "fair share" is really the efficient share. (Actually, in a society where the distribution of the federal tax burden is on a progressive basis and where some income redistribution is an avowed goal, a state's share of tax payments is no guide to its "fair" share of expenditures even if efficiency is not a goal.) But many of the complaints about the regional distribution come when there is general unemployment, and it is realized that defense orders can be a net addition to demand where they are directed. In those circumstances, it is understandable how the benefits of defense come to be identified with the receipt of contracts, rather than with the efficient production of goods.

Defense Procurement in Labor Surplus Areas

The impact—or lack of it—of defense spending on "depressed areas" is an important policy issue, since "pockets" of structural unemployment have been recognized as a major long-term problem. The troubles of some areas can be traced partly to the closing of military installations. In addition, the military services purchase such a wide variety of items, and in such large volume, that defense contracts have appealed to many as a partial solution to the problem.

As early as 1951, directives from the President and the Secretary of Defense ordered procurement officers in all parts of the Federal government to take steps to increase procurement in labor surplus areas.[5] The present authority which permits the establishment of artificial advantages is Defense Manpower Policy No. 4, issued by the Director of Defense Mobilization in March 1952, and amended in the summer of that year to allow for matching of low bids by contractors in labor surplus areas; after a low bid was determined, contractors in such areas could get the order by matching that bid. Congress criticized this system, however, and in 1953 an amendment changed the advantage to the "set-aside" type, meaning that a certain portion of a procurement was to be reserved for contractors who would perform or cause to be performed a substantial

[5] This paragraph and the next two are largely based on material in *Impact of Defense Spending on Labor Surplus Areas, 1962,* Hearings, *passim.*

TABLE 29. Military Prime Contract Awards in Labor Surplus Areas, 1953–64

(Millions of dollars)

Period	Total Procurement[a]	Awards in All Labor Surplus Areas[b]				Number of Major Surplus Areas[c]
		Total Amount	Percent of Total Procurement	Preference Awards	Percent of Total Procurement	
FY 1953	28,394	829	2.9	23	.1	
FY 1954	13,868	551	4.0	8	.1	
FY 1955	15,471	1,466	9.5	48	.3	
FY 1956	16,964	645	3.8	4	d	
FY 1957	18,575	401	2.2	11	.1	
FY 1958	21,116	3,791	18.0	37	.2	
FY 1959	22,000	9,345	42.5	96	.4	
FY 1960	20,505	1,958	9.6	22	.1	
FY 1961	22,181	6,342	28.6	50	.2	
FY 1962	25,061	7,389	29.5	106	.4	
FY 1963	25,091	3,838	15.3	138	.5	
FY 1964	25,196	4,115	16.3	173	.7	
July–Sept. 1957	3,086	68	2.2	—	d	24
Oct.–Dec. 1957	4,729	89	1.9	1	d	24
Jan.–Mar. 1958	5,016	1,122	22.4	2		70
Apr.–June 1958	8,285	2,512	30.3	34	.5	86
July–Sept. 1958	4,218	2,205	52.2	22	.5	89
Oct.–Dec. 1958	5,573	3,227	57.9	24	.4	83
Jan.–Mar. 1959	4,782	1,708	35.7	22	.5	74
Apr.–June 1959	7,426	2,206	29.7	27	.4	60
July–Sept. 1959	4,384	854	19.5	8	.2	35
Oct.–Dec. 1959	4,614	264	5.7	4	.1	32
Jan.–Mar. 1960	4,780	289	6.0	4	.1	33
Apr.–June 1960	6,726	551	8.2	5	.1	35
July–Sept. 1960	5,054	407	8.0	4	.1	42
Oct.–Dec. 1960	4,567	397	8.7	5	.1	51
Jan.–Mar. 1961	5,325	1,604	30.1	7	.1	101
Apr.–June 1961	7,244	3,933	54.4	34	.5	96
July–Sept. 1961	4,783	2,008	42.0	12	.3	72
Oct.–Dec. 1961	6,398	1,855	29.0	27	.4	60
Jan.–Mar. 1962	6,909	2,091	30.3	35	.5	63
Apr.–June 1962	6,970	1,435	20.6	32	.5	51
July–Sept. 1962	4,872	827	17.0	18	.4	44
Oct.–Dec. 1962	6,600	839	12.7	18	.3	41
Jan.–Mar. 1963	6,452	854	13.2	43	.7	48
Apr.–June 1963	7,167	1,318	18.4	59	.8	39
July–Sept. 1963	6,708	860	12.8	34	.5	37
Oct.–Dec. 1963	5,077	721	14.2	43	.8	38
Jan.–Mar. 1964	6,104	1,115	18.3	31	.5	40
Apr.–June 1964	7,306	1,419	19.4	65	.9	37
July–Sept. 1964	6,089	1,296	21.3	37	.6	31
Oct.–Dec. 1964	4,869	930	19.1	28	.6	29

Source: U. S. Department of Defense, *Military Prime Contract Awards in Areas of Substantial Unemployment* (quarterly issues, 1957–64).

[a] From 1956 on, total prime contracts for work in the United States amounting to $10,000 or more; before 1956, total prime contracts for work in the United States. The fiscal year 1964 and later figures include Defense Department civil functions (rivers and harbors) as well.

[b] If an area was classified as labor surplus for only part of the period, only awards during that part of the period are included. Prior to January 1, 1958, data include only awards of $25,000 or more for supplies and equipment; subsequently, they include action of $10,000 or more for supplies, equipment, services, and construction.

[c] Through fiscal 1961, quarterly data are as of the end of September, November, March, and May; in fiscal 1962, as of the end of the quarter in all cases.

d Less than .05 percent.

part of the work in a labor surplus area. Beginning with the 1954 appropriations bills, Congress consistently barred the payment of more than the lowest competitive price obtainable merely to relieve "economic dislocation." This means that the policy of set-asides may not be used to split an order into such small lots that costs are raised.

Defense Manpower Policy No. 4 also establishes preference in the case of tie bids; a bid from a labor surplus area is automatically preferred over one from an area without a labor surplus.

As amended in 1960, the Policy incorporates the congressional barrier against price differentials, establishes preferential treatment for *persistent* labor surplus areas over other surplus areas, and calls on procurement agencies to favor prime contractors who will perform work in labor surplus areas or subcontract to vendors in them.

Table 29 presents data on contracting in labor surplus areas. The percentage of all contract value was low except during recessions, when the number of areas in the labor surplus category rose. Even in recession, the *preference* mechanism did little to raise procurement in such areas; most of the rise in the percentage came from contracts which would have been granted to the areas anyway. Preference awards never reached even 1 percent of total procurement in the periods covered in the table.

In fiscal years 1961 and 1962, the percentage of contract value to labor surplus areas rose greatly over the previous year. But awards in twenty-one large, normally important procurement areas accounted for about 80 percent of the awards, and there were other normally important procurement areas which went on the list. Just eight labor market areas—Los Angeles-Long Beach, San Diego, San Jose, Wichita, Philadelphia, Detroit, Seattle, and St. Louis—accounted for well over half of all labor surplus awards.

There had been little success by 1964 in the use of defense contracts to alleviate areas of *persistent* labor surplus. For fiscal years 1963 and 1964, these areas received 3.4 percent of procurement each year but preference awards accounted for less than 0.4 percent of total procurement in 1963, and only 0.5 percent in 1964.

Even though it must be concluded that official mechanisms for alleviating specific pockets of labor surplus have had relatively little effect, their effect may have been greater than available data indicate. Although certain areas account for most of the awards, they

might not have received *as much* procurement had they not been on
the labor surplus list. And the absence of preference awards is not
inconsistent with giving unofficial advantage by procurement
officers. Since negotiation is so important a part of the process of
awarding contracts, preference can be given without use of the formal mechanism.

Several factors prevent widespread use of the official mechanisms. Tie bids are rare. The set-aside provision is hampered by the
difficulty of splitting orders into parts large enough to be economi-
cal. Set-asides are also troublesome for procurement officers, who
perhaps are also accustomed to negotiating with established sources.

The Kennedy administration made new efforts to use the official
set-aside procedure, and the volume of contracts granted under
them consequently rose. When the number of major labor surplus
areas declined with recovery in the latter half of 1961 and in 1962,
the awards under the set-aside procedure actually rose, and the total
labor surplus percentage fell less than in previous recoveries.[6] New
efforts were also made to channel subcontracts into labor surplus
areas, but these measures did not produce dramatic changes. Writ-
ing in 1962, one student of the problem ventured the opinion that:

> Neither statistics nor observation offer proof that the impact of the
> Federal efforts under the Defense Manpower Policy No. 4 order have
> been of major significance. The reluctance of Congress, the President,
> and the policymaking and operating agency personnel to mount a mas-
> sive offensive against the chronic disease of unemployment has pre-
> cluded impressive results. While the principle of Federal responsibility for
> the achievement of full employment has been given lip service by all re-
> sponsible officials, the wholehearted effort required to establish adequate
> machinery and to implement the policies adopted has been lacking.[7]

Table 29 shows a large rise in the volume of labor surplus awards
in the last half of 1964 as compared with the same six months in
1963. Although the preference arrangements are obviously not the

---

[6] Statement of Ron M. Linton, in *ibid.,* p. 50. For a limited time in 1962-64,
the set-aside procedures were somewhat liberalized on a trial basis, but this
ended in February 1964. See the notes to the report by the U.S. Department of
Defense, *Prime Contract Awards in Areas of Substantial Unemployment* (March
1964).

[7] Conley Dillon, "Government Purchases and Depressed Areas," *Challenge,*
Vol. 10 (July 1962), p. 14.

cause, this rise may be the result of more effort to expand procurement in labor surplus areas. However, about two-thirds of the rise can be traced to rises for just three areas—Seattle (newly added to the labor surplus list in October 1963), Philadelphia, and Paterson-Clifton-Passaic, New Jersey. These three areas are normally areas of heavy procurement, so the rises may not have been influenced much by their being labor surplus areas.

There simply is no capacity to produce for defense procurement in some labor surplus areas, even if a reasonable price differential were allowed. This is especially true for small areas with a persistent labor surplus. Capacity must be created first, and it is not always feasible for defense procurement to wait until capacity comes into being. While many would favor a price differential, either on grounds of real social costs and benefits or on grounds of income redistribution, in the long run there are more efficient ways to rehabilitate depressed areas. Such areas should be assisted by grants and loans to finance worker retraining and new social overhead capital, so that the resources can be redeveloped into their most productive capability. Real cost grounds may justify use of defense orders to aid depressed areas in the short run, but in the long run such areas may become even more valuable to the economy if they undertake other lines of production. This conclusion is supported by the fact that the volume and composition of defense procurement are uncertain, which means that labor surplus areas will benefit more if their *general* productivity is redeveloped.

CHAPTER X

Conclusion

THE PRIMARY CONCLUSIONS were presented in Chapter VI, where each state and region was classified by its dependence on defense income in 1962 and the relative stimulus given to growth by defense income in the 1952-62 period. That discussion showed that there is a wide spectrum of cases, that not all rapidly growing states can trace much of their growth to defense activity, and that some states have grown at a rapid rate despite a slow rate of increase in their defense income. Income generated by defense demand has been a significant factor in the growth of many states, but it has been only one factor.

On the basis of the model and estimates presented in this study, I believe that growth in many states would have been significantly different had the distribution of defense purchases been different. The estimates and the accuracy of the model are of course subject to error. But it is clear that the simple model fitted the data well, and that for only a few important states were the alternative estimates of defense purchases so different as to make questionable the use of the middle value. Even where there was considerable spread, the estimated *growth* of defense income is probably more accurate than the absolute amounts for any one year. The possible error, then, is not great enough to vitiate the general conclusions.

Some feel that the composition of the defense bill of goods has stabilized and that further dramatic changes are unlikely. But I believe the possibility is great enough to force explicit consideration of the issue.

To proclaim the narrow criterion of "efficiency" or "least cost" is not to dispose of the issue; it only reflects one policy choice, which must be justified by value judgments expressed in the political process. I agree that the efficiency criterion is the best one, but I feel that in the past it was adopted more or less automatically, without the results it implied being sufficiently well understood. To some extent, this was a result of the inability to foresee a general slackening of growth and the relative decline of the "goods sector" in the economy in the late 1950's, for these occurrences surely contributed in a general way to difficulties in those areas which also suffered the *specific* loss of defense business.

These same developments also affect the validity of the choice of the efficiency criterion, as opposed to, say, a "fair share" rule. The least-cost rule is most attractive under conditions of generally full employment, if other government policies foster economic growth and eliminate pockets of structural unemployment. Surely the absence of some other policies has encouraged criticism of the actual distribution of defense spending in the past. In the best of times, the defense budget is large enough, varied enough, and allows enough discretion in the placement of contracts to require a full consideration of the regional effects. In less favorable times, many have naturally considered the defense budget a tool for achieving goals apart from efficiency. Those who oppose this and insist on the least-cost rule must also insist on other economic policies which apply more appropriate instruments to economic problems.

Most present discussions of the regional distribution of defense activity arise from conjecture about disarmament or some less drastic reduction in defense expenditures—rather than from an historical analysis such as this. But the possibility of disarmament greatly reinforces the above observations, for it presents the possibility of a drastic change in the composition of demand. Even if the total budgetary requirements of an international policing system would be little less than those under the present system, the new bill of goods might be very different. As of now, only a start has been made in planning for national adjustment to disarmament, let alone the regional adjustments. Just as in the previous shifts, the regional problem would be partly a *company* problem. In this light, a 1963 report by *The New York Times* is not encouraging. It found that defense contractors in general were then making little preparation to cope with the impact of possible arms control or disarmament.[1] While more progress seems to have been made since then, this is still a matter of concern.

If the composition of defense equipment changes in the future, either because of arms control or of changes in defense technology, the federal government will face pressure to ease specific hardships. Certain interests would undoubtedly urge abandonment of the least-cost rule in procurement, and this pressure would be the greater the less adequate other adjustment policies appeared to be. Areas now supporting the least-cost principle most vigorously might call for use of other criteria, and vice versa. The dependence of many areas on defense would insure this, especially after the lessons of the post-Korean shifts in distribution. In those circumstances, policymakers must explicitly compare the economic gains from efficient procurement with the values placed on the estimated impact on regions and industries adversely affected.

The parameters estimated for each state in the testing of the simple growth model overestimate the adverse effect on personal income of a given reduction in defense income. There is certainly a "ratchet effect," which means that a downward response is less pronounced than an upward one. This would seem to be true even in the absence of offsetting government policies, although it is less true as the period of time before defense income is replaced by some other demand increases in length. The percentages showing the relative importance of defense income in total exogenous income, however, give a rough idea of the ranking of effects of a cut in defense purchases distributed in the same way as were total purchases in 1962. More detailed estimates would require knowledge of policies designed to cushion the impact of a cut, new needs for arms control, if any, and the composition of the new demand which presumably would take up most of the slack caused by reductions in arms spending.

[1] "Defense Industry Lacks Plans for Civilian Production," *The New York Times,* August 16, 1963, p. 31.

General Appendix Tables

TABLE A-1. Estimated Annual Defense Purchases, by State and Region, 1951-62[a]

(Millions of dollars)

State or Region	1951	1952	1953	1954	1955	1956	1957	1958	1959	1960	1961	1962
Maine	109	169	172	180	156	177	186	218	195	181	207	217
New Hampshire	82	108	103	102	89	96	108	118	141	159	178	179
Vermont	28	58	55	43	32	31	36	45	37	37	39	40
Massachusetts	956	1,255	1,315	996	909	1,010	1,195	1,290	1,534	1,543	1,690	1,728
Connecticut	815	1,077	1,134	1,186	1,019	1,137	1,220	986	1,019	1,089	1,206	1,290
Rhode Island	212	281	284	234	216	213	207	213	217	199	217	247
New England	2,202	2,944	3,063	2,741	2,421	2,668	2,954	2,869	3,140	3,210	3,540	3,698
New York	3,164	4,318	4,204	3,718	3,184	3,038	3,383	3,347	3,444	3,423	3,647	3,729
New Jersey	1,318	1,918	2,146	1,596	1,582	1,526	1,616	1,583	1,764	1,702	1,818	1,977
Pennsylvania	1,598	2,206	2,205	1,741	1,642	1,708	1,847	1,748	1,795	1,789	1,990	2,191
Middle Atlantic	6,081	8,442	8,555	7,054	6,410	6,272	6,845	6,679	7,006	6,911	7,455	7,897
Ohio	1,624	2,410	2,379	1,726	1,694	1,812	2,082	1,882	1,962	1,824	1,884	2,101
Indiana	1,053	1,431	1,324	875	819	768	853	749	809	744	850	958
Illinois	1,531	2,154	2,304	1,774	1,725	1,729	1,693	1,531	1,551	1,481	1,610	1,718
Michigan	1,605	2,967	2,445	971	830	894	1,088	1,154	1,217	1,193	1,269	1,401
Wisconsin	470	699	672	411	342	370	402	407	440	429	480	530
East North Central	6,285	9,660	9,123	5,756	5,413	5,571	6,120	5,723	5,979	5,671	6,090	6,705
Minnesota	225	346	379	286	244	260	296	299	324	318	339	394
Iowa	175	265	287	196	202	193	219	213	252	244	262	277
Missouri	531	814	940	660	571	687	709	780	836	713	783	868
North Dakota	13	15	14	14	19	20	37	32	23	39	72	82
South Dakota	30	46	47	45	45	45	45	51	66	54	82	97
Nebraska	102	152	166	129	125	125	132	145	167	179	191	197
Kansas	348	489	1,026	660	490	653	648	785	712	649	659	654
West North Central	1,423	2,126	2,857	1,989	1,696	1,983	2,090	2,305	2,380	2,194	2,385	2,570
Delaware	46	128	65	121	98	82	118	142	130	111	109	118
Maryland	799	1,062	1,281	967	1,004	1,074	1,133	1,082	1,169	1,090	1,167	1,222
District of Columbia	355	403	318	315	341	346	317	320	324	321	308	374

152

Virginia	1,073	1,284	1,301	1,208	1,141	1,122	1,222	1,189	1,317	1,357	1,461	1,555
West Virginia	97	125	139	109	94	95	100	113	118	114	127	172
North Carolina	500	625	632	564	598	612	696	753	703	677	743	810
South Carolina	347	410	392	354	328	340	372	371	403	403	425	465
Georgia	483	745	807	743	699	705	745	766	767	740	785	944
Florida	355	515	566	583	562	639	731	828	895	937	1,063	1,099
South Atlantic	4,054	5,295	5,499	4,965	4,865	5,012	5,434	5,566	5,829	5,750	6,188	6,762
Kentucky	346	418	421	344	366	308	324	337	348	357	391	425
Tennessee	238	372	396	286	286	305	326	330	345	339	378	427
Alabama	319	441	509	424	430	470	537	544	544	517	529	579
Mississippi	141	184	192	224	192	182	207	214	232	237	251	284
East South Central	1,045	1,412	1,516	1,277	1,271	1,267	1,392	1,423	1,470	1,447	1,548	1,713
Arkansas	104	153	165	150	145	147	159	142	129	114	168	194
Oklahoma	247	403	507	360	370	385	412	424	421	405	410	446
Louisiana	250	374	419	310	298	342	394	355	341	310	334	440
Texas	1,293	1,773	1,990	1,691	1,772	1,847	2,190	2,177	2,168	2,111	2,152	2,254
West South Central	1,893	2,702	3,079	2,514	2,585	2,722	3,155	3,097	3,056	2,939	3,064	3,335
Montana	27	36	39	35	40	48	47	55	61	61	95	100
Idaho	27	47	45	41	36	41	41	46	50	60	59	64
Wyoming	35	43	44	44	43	51	51	37	46	37	38	72
Colorado	194	249	250	271	261	318	395	387	418	471	582	658
Utah	113	143	150	133	138	140	152	178	251	286	355	448
Nevada	26	38	52	54	52	54	59	56	57	57	64	61
Arizona	87	136	166	184	192	244	280	314	296	325	307	338
New Mexico	103	143	168	184	180	170	184	209	213	218	206	218
Mountain	613	834	917	948	942	1,064	1,207	1,279	1,390	1,517	1,706	1,957
Washington	829	1,055	1,467	1,281	1,100	965	1,044	1,188	1,268	1,097	1,180	1,378
Oregon	151	192	177	138	131	132	136	140	159	150	161	169
California	3,886	5,061	5,711	5,112	4,975	5,412	5,843	6,232	6,828	6,728	7,346	7,988
Pacific	4,866	6,305	7,354	6,530	6,203	6,508	7,021	7,558	8,255	7,974	8,689	9,535
Hawaii	99[b]	125[b]	129[b]	129[b]	145[b]	186[c]	204[c]	200[c]	313	325	333	351
Alaska	112[b]	137[b]	148[b]	147[b]	149[b]	206[c]	224[c]	195[c]	225	239	223	220
United States	28,668	39,983	42,234	34,045	32,102	33,457	36,646	36,889	39,044	38,176	41,209	44,738

Sources: Calculated from the sources listed for Tables 5 and 11.
a β=.2.
b Includes only military payrolls.
c Includes only military payrolls and estimated procurement.

TABLE A-2. Alternative Estimates of Annual Procurement Purchases, by State and Region, 1951–62

(Dollar amounts in millions)

State or Region	1951						1952					
	Estimated Purchases			v, in Percent			Estimated Purchases			v, in Percent		
	β=.3	β=.2	β=.1	β=.3	β=.2	β=.1	β=.3	β=.2	β=.1	β=.3	β=.2	β=.1
Maine	59	67	76	.33	.37	.42	103	113	124	.38	.42	.46
New Hampshire	45	50	54	.25	.28	.30	59	68	76	.22	.25	.28
Vermont	22	23	25	.12	.13	.14	51	50	49	.19	.18	.18
Massachusetts	662	662	661	3.68	3.68	3.67	872	886	899	3.23	3.28	3.33
Connecticut	808	767	727	4.49	4.26	4.04	1,077	1,025	972	3.99	3.80	3.60
Rhode Island	90	103	113	.50	.57	.63	132	147	162	.49	.54	.60
New England	1,687	1,672	1,656	9.37	9.29	9.20	2,292	2,286	2,279	8.49	8.47	8.44
New York	2,655	2,649	2,642	14.75	14.72	14.68	3,629	3,642	3,655	13.44	13.49	13.54
New Jersey	1,069	1,016	963	5.94	5.64	5.35	1,582	1,531	1,480	5.86	5.67	5.48
Pennsylvania	1,040	1,138	1,235	5.78	6.32	6.86	1,499	1,650	1,801	5.55	6.11	6.67
Middle Atlantic	4,765	4,804	4,842	26.47	26.69	26.90	6,710	6,823	6,936	24.85	25.27	25.69
Ohio	1,240	1,309	1,378	6.89	7.27	7.66	1,976	2,039	2,101	7.32	7.55	7.78
Indiana	940	908	877	5.22	5.04	4.87	1,296	1,252	1,207	4.80	4.64	4.47
Illinois	1,156	1,163	1,170	6.42	6.46	6.50	1,669	1,706	1,743	6.18	6.32	6.46
Michigan	1,465	1,466	1,467	8.14	8.14	8.15	2,878	2,781	2,684	10.66	10.30	9.94
Wisconsin	355	396	436	1.97	2.20	2.42	575	624	672	2.13	2.31	2.49
East North Central	5,157	5,242	5,328	28.65	29.12	29.60	8,394	8,402	8,410	31.09	31.12	31.15
Minnesota	178	189	200	.99	1.05	1.11	289	302	316	1.07	1.12	1.17
Iowa	148	153	157	.82	.85	.87	230	235	240	.85	.87	.89
Missouri	344	349	353	1.91	1.94	1.96	653	645	637	2.42	2.39	2.36
North Dakota	2	3	4	.01	.01	.02	3	4	5	.01	.02	.02
South Dakota	4	4	4	.02	.02	.02	8	11	14	.03	.04	.05
Nebraska	52	53	54	.29	.30	.30	92	95	97	.34	.35	.36
Kansas	292	246	200	1.62	1.37	1.11	402	346	289	1.49	1.28	1.07
West North Central	1,021	997	973	5.67	5.54	5.41	1,677	1,638	1,598	6.21	6.07	5.92

154

Kentucky	79	88	97	.44	.49	.54	113	128	143	.42	.47	.53
Tennessee	106	128	151	.59	.71	.84	205	239	273	.76	.88	1.01
Alabama	106	120	133	.59	.67	.75	170	185	200	.63	.68	.74
Mississippi	32	36	41	.18	.20	.23	68	73	78	.25	.27	.29
East South Central	322	373	424	1.79	2.07	2.36	554	622	691	2.05	2.30	2.56
Arkansas	23	30	36	.13	.17	.20	62	69	76	.23	.26	.28
Oklahoma	54	59	65	.30	.33	.36	165	166	167	.61	.62	.62
Louisiana	106	112	117	.59	.62	.65	176	184	192	.65	.68	.71
Texas	515	486	457	2.86	2.70	2.54	796	778	760	2.95	2.88	2.82
West South Central	700	686	673	3.89	3.82	3.74	1,199	1,196	1,193	4.44	4.43	4.42
Delaware	27	33	40	.15	.18	.22	105	113	122	.39	.42	.45
Maryland	448	405	362	2.49	2.25	2.01	599	551	502	2.22	2.04	1.86
District of Columbia	95	96	97	.53	.53	.54	127	129	130	.47	.48	.48
Virginia	194	198	202	1.08	1.10	1.12	273	279	286	1.01	1.03	1.06
West Virginia	61	73	85	.34	.40	.47	78	99	119	.29	.37	.44
North Carolina	196	223	250	1.09	1.24	1.39	267	308	348	.99	1.14	1.29
South Carolina	70	88	106	.39	.49	.59	111	138	165	.41	.51	.61
Georgia	124	141	158	.69	.78	.88	316	336	355	1.17	1.24	1.31
Florida	59	63	67	.33	.35	.37	108	115	122	.40	.42	.45
South Atlantic	1,272	1,319	1,366	7.06	7.32	7.59	1,985	2,066	2,148	7.35	7.65	7.96
Montana	7	9	11	.04	.05	.06	11	14	16	.04	.05	.06
Idaho	11	13	16	.06	.07	.09	14	19	24	.05	.07	.09
Wyoming	5	5	5	.03	.03	.03	5	6	8	.02	.02	.03
Colorado	38	44	50	.21	.25	.28	59	68	78	.22	.25	.29
Utah	14	18	22	.08	.10	.12	22	27	32	.08	.10	.12
Nevada	4	4	4	.02	.02	.02	8	8	8	.03	.03	.03
Arizona	25	25	25	.14	.14	.14	49	46	43	.18	.17	.16
New Mexico	29	23	18	.16	.13	.10	41	34	27	.15	.12	.10
Mountain	131	142	153	.73	.79	.85	208	221	235	.77	.82	.87
Washington	470	445	419	2.61	2.47	2.33	635	617	598	2.35	2.28	2.21
Oregon	90	105	121	.50	.58	.67	113	136	159	.42	.50	.59
California	2,387	2,216	2,045	13.26	12.31	11.36	3,237	2,996	2,754	11.99	11.10	10.20
Pacific	2,947	2,766	2,585	16.37	15.36	14.36	3,983	3,746	3,510	14.75	13.88	13.00
Hawaii	—	—	—	—	—	—	—	—	—	—	—	—
Alaska	—	—	—	—	—	—	—	—	—	—	—	—
United States	18,000	18,000	18,000	100.00	100.00	100.00	27,000	27,000	27,000	100.00	100.00	100.00

TABLE A-2—Continued

(Dollar amounts in millions)

State or Region	1953 Estimated Purchases β=.3	β=.2	β=.1	1953 v, in Percent β=.3	β=.2	β=.1	1954 Estimated Purchases β=.3	β=.2	β=.1	1954 v, in Percent β=.3	β=.2	β=.1
Maine	100	109	118	.34	.37	.40	100	106	113	.46	.49	.52
New Hampshire	59	66	74	.20	.22	.25	56	62	67	.26	.29	.31
Vermont	47	47	47	.16	.16	.16	32	34	36	.15	.16	.17
Massachusetts	944	958	971	3.21	3.26	3.30	664	675	686	3.06	3.11	3.16
Connecticut	1,135	1,076	1,017	3.86	3.66	3.46	1,185	1,133	1,081	5.46	5.22	4.98
Rhode Island	129	145	162	.44	.49	.55	74	90	106	.34	.42	.49
New England	2,414	2,401	2,388	8.21	8.17	8.12	2,113	2,100	2,087	9.74	9.68	9.61
New York	3,554	3,550	3,546	12.09	12.07	12.06	3,138	3,104	3,070	14.46	14.30	14.15
New Jersey	1,790	1,740	1,691	6.09	5.92	5.75	1,273	1,221	1,169	5.87	5.63	5.39
Pennsylvania	1,523	1,670	1,817	5.18	5.68	6.18	1,150	1,252	1,355	5.30	5.77	6.24
Middle Atlantic	6,868	6,960	7,053	23.36	23.67	23.99	5,560	5,576	5,592	25.62	25.70	25.77
Ohio	1,929	2,006	2,084	6.56	6.82	7.09	1,322	1,388	1,453	6.09	6.40	6.70
Indiana	1,176	1,142	1,107	4.00	3.88	3.76	751	737	723	3.46	3.40	3.33
Illinois	1,882	1,913	1,943	6.40	6.51	6.61	1,338	1,365	1,391	6.17	6.29	6.41
Michigan	2,326	2,287	2,249	7.91	7.78	7.65	692	832	973	3.19	3.84	4.48
Wisconsin	571	623	674	1.94	2.12	2.29	312	363	414	1.44	1.67	1.89
East North Central	7,883	7,969	8,056	26.81	27.10	27.40	4,415	4,684	4,952	20.35	21.58	22.82
Minnesota	320	334	349	1.09	1.13	1.18	226	238	250	1.04	1.10	1.15
Iowa	235	242	249	.80	.83	.85	163	166	169	.75	.77	.78
Missouri	770	756	741	2.62	2.57	2.52	464	458	451	2.14	2.11	2.08
North Dakota	3	4	6	.01	.01	.02	4	4	4	.02	.02	.02
South Dakota	9	11	12	.03	.04	.04	7	9	11	.03	.04	.05
Nebraska	103	104	106	.35	.35	.36	56	59	61	.26	.27	.28
Kansas	897	849	800	3.05	2.89	2.72	525	482	439	2.42	2.22	2.03
West North Central	2,334	2,298	2,261	7.94	7.82	7.69	1,443	1,415	1,386	6.65	6.52	6.39

Kentucky	129	147	165	.44	.50	.56	95	111	128	.44	.51	.59
Tennessee	232	265	297	.79	.90	1.01	137	161	184	.63	.74	.85
Alabama	222	238	253	.75	.81	.86	169	181	193	.78	.83	.89
Mississippi	74	79	85	.25	.27	.29	104	106	109	.48	.49	.50
East South Central	656	727	798	2.23	2.47	2.71	503	558	613	2.32	2.57	2.83
Arkansas	62	71	79	.21	.24	.27	52	58	65	.24	.27	.30
Oklahoma	273	272	270	.93	.93	.92	132	125	119	.61	.58	.55
Louisiana	221	225	229	.75	.77	.78	150	153	156	.69	.71	.72
Texas	1,017	995	973	3.46	3.38	3.31	692	667	643	3.19	3.08	2.96
West South Central	1,573	1,561	1,549	5.35	5.31	5.27	1,025	1,005	985	4.72	4.63	4.54
Delaware	41	47	53	.14	.16	.18	89	96	104	.41	.44	.48
Maryland	815	767	718	2.77	2.61	2.44	506	461	416	2.33	2.12	1.92
District of Columbia	74	75	76	.25	.25	.26	72	73	74	.33	.33	.34
Virginia	282	291	300	.96	.99	1.02	273	275	278	1.26	1.27	1.28
West Virginia	94	116	138	.32	.39	.47	69	85	100	.32	.39	.46
North Carolina	276	318	359	.94	1.08	1.22	215	241	267	.99	1.11	1.23
South Carolina	115	145	176	.39	.49	.60	76	98	119	.35	.45	.55
Georgia	400	416	432	1.36	1.42	1.47	293	301	308	1.35	1.39	1.42
Florida	126	134	141	.43	.46	.48	128	134	141	.59	.62	.65
South Atlantic	2,220	2,307	2,393	7.55	7.85	8.14	1,720	1,765	1,810	7.93	8.13	8.34
Montana	15	17	18	.05	.06	.06	9	12	15	.04	.06	.07
Idaho	18	22	26	.06	.08	.09	15	18	22	.07	.08	.10
Wyoming	6	7	9	.02	.02	.03	7	7	7	.03	.03	.03
Colorado	68	76	85	.23	.26	.29	56	60	65	.26	.28	.30
Utah	29	32	35	.10	.11	.12	22	27	33	.10	.13	.15
Nevada	15	15	15	.05	.05	.05	11	12	13	.05	.06	.06
Arizona	88	79	71	.30	.27	.24	93	85	78	.43	.39	.36
New Mexico	50	41	32	.17	.14	.11	63	54	46	.29	.25	.21
Mountain	288	291	294	.98	.99	1.00	276	277	278	1.27	1.28	1.28
Washington	1,072	1,047	1,023	3.65	3.56	3.48	914	879	844	4.21	4.05	3.89
Oregon	106	129	153	.36	.44	.52	76	94	113	.35	.43	.52
California	3,990	3,713	3,437	13.57	12.63	11.69	3,654	3,349	3,043	16.84	15.43	14.02
Pacific	5,166	4,888	4,610	17.57	16.62	15.68	4,644	4,321	3,998	21.40	19.91	18.42
Hawaii	—	—	—	—	—	—	—	—	—	—	—	—
Alaska	—	—	—	—	—	—	—	—	—	—	—	—
United States	29,400	29,400	29,400	100.00	100.00	100.00	21,700	21,700	21,700	100.00	100.00	100.00

TABLE A-2—Continued

(Dollar amounts in millions)

State or Region	1955 Estimated Purchases			1955 v, in Percent			1956 Estimated Purchases			1956 v, in Percent		
	$\beta=.3$	$\beta=.2$	$\beta=.1$	$\beta=.3$	$\beta=.2$	$\beta=.1$	$\beta=.3$	$\beta=.2$	$\beta=.1$	$\beta=.3$	$\beta=.2$	$\beta=.1$
Maine	77	82	87	.39	.42	.44	94	100	106	.45	.48	.51
New Hampshire	49	54	59	.25	.28	.31	48	53	58	.23	.25	.28
Vermont	24	25	26	.12	.12	.13	19	23	27	.09	.11	.13
Massachusetts	582	587	591	2.95	2.98	3.00	683	686	689	3.28	3.30	3.31
Connecticut	1,015	962	910	5.15	4.88	4.62	1,140	1,077	1,014	5.48	5.18	4.88
Rhode Island	57	71	85	.29	.36	.43	53	67	82	.26	.32	.39
New England	1,802	1,780	1,758	9.13	9.03	8.93	2,040	2,009	1,978	9.81	9.66	9.51
New York	2,563	2,547	2,531	13.01	12.93	12.85	2,414	2,409	2,404	11.61	11.58	11.56
New Jersey	1,286	1,235	1,184	6.53	6.27	6.01	1,242	1,193	1,144	5.97	5.74	5.50
Pennsylvania	1,042	1,141	1,241	5.29	5.80	6.30	1,099	1,209	1,318	5.29	5.81	6.34
Middle Atlantic	4,891	4,925	4,958	24.83	25.00	25.17	4,756	4,811	4,867	22.86	23.13	23.40
Ohio	1,269	1,335	1,402	6.44	6.78	7.12	1,355	1,434	1,514	6.52	6.90	7.28
Indiana	713	700	687	3.62	3.55	3.49	652	644	636	3.13	3.10	3.06
Illinois	1,294	1,316	1,338	6.57	6.68	6.79	1,294	1,320	1,345	6.22	6.34	6.47
Michigan	535	684	833	2.72	3.47	4.23	596	742	888	2.86	3.57	4.27
Wisconsin	248	296	345	1.26	1.50	1.75	267	317	366	1.29	1.52	1.76
East North Central	4,062	4,334	4,605	20.62	22.00	23.38	4,162	4,456	4,749	20.01	21.42	22.83
Minnesota	185	197	209	.94	1.00	1.06	197	210	222	.95	1.01	1.07
Iowa	156	159	162	.79	.81	.82	145	149	153	.70	.72	.74
Missouri	376	376	376	1.91	1.91	1.91	492	495	497	2.37	2.38	2.39
North Dakota	8	9	10	.04	.04	.05	10	10	10	.05	.05	.05
South Dakota	8	9	10	.04	.05	.05	10	11	12	.05	.06	.06
Nebraska	47	50	53	.24	.26	.27	44	47	50	.21	.23	.24
Kansas	351	313	276	1.78	1.59	1.40	508	469	430	2.44	2.25	2.07
West North Central	1,131	1,113	1,095	5.74	5.66	5.56	1,405	1,391	1,377	6.76	6.69	6.62

	Number			Percent			Number			Percent		
Kentucky	99	114	128	.50	.58	.65	89	106	123	.43	.51	.59
Tennessee	132	155	177	.67	.79	.90	142	166	189	.68	.80	.91
Alabama	173	184	195	.88	.93	.99	187	197	207	.90	.95	.99
Mississippi	73	75	77	.37	.38	.39	66	68	70	.32	.34	.36
East South Central	475	525	575	2.41	2.66	2.92	484	539	593	2.33	2.59	2.85
Arkansas	47	53	59	.24	.27	.30	35	44	52	.17	.21	.25
Oklahoma	148	139	130	.75	.70	.66	150	142	135	.72	.68	.65
Louisiana	160	165	169	.81	.84	.86	157	165	173	.75	.79	.83
Texas	796	776	756	4.04	3.94	3.84	872	841	810	4.19	4.04	3.89
West South Central	1,150	1,133	1,115	5.84	5.75	5.66	1,215	1,193	1,170	5.84	5.73	5.63
Delaware	59	67	75	.30	.34	.38	37	46	56	.18	.22	.27
Maryland	526	477	427	2.67	2.42	2.17	586	539	491	2.82	2.59	2.36
District of Columbia	71	72	73	.36	.37	.37	71	72	73	.34	.35	.35
Virginia	223	228	232	1.13	1.16	1.18	198	205	212	.95	.98	1.02
West Virginia	57	72	87	.29	.36	.44	56	72	87	.27	.35	.42
North Carolina	252	275	299	1.28	1.40	1.52	273	300	327	1.31	1.44	1.57
South Carolina	69	89	108	.35	.45	.55	69	91	112	.33	.44	.54
Georgia	276	278	280	1.40	1.41	1.42	294	296	298	1.41	1.42	1.43
Florida	130	136	142	.66	.69	.72	158	165	171	.76	.79	.82
South Atlantic	1,663	1,694	1,725	8.44	8.60	8.76	1,742	1,783	1,825	8.37	8.57	8.78
Montana	16	18	20	.08	.09	.10	19	22	25	.09	.10	.12
Idaho	12	16	20	.06	.08	.10	15	19	23	.07	.09	.11
Wyoming	6	7	8	.03	.03	.04	6	7	8	.03	.04	.04
Colorado	51	56	61	.26	.28	.31	99	101	103	.48	.49	.50
Utah	26	30	35	.13	.16	.18	30	34	39	.15	.17	.19
Nevada	10	11	12	.05	.06	.06	10	11	12	.05	.05	.06
Arizona	87	77	67	.44	.37	.34	143	126	109	.69	.61	.53
New Mexico	65	55	45	.33	.28	.23	43	41	39	.21	.20	.19
Mountain	274	270	266	1.39	1.37	1.35	362	359	357	1.74	1.72	1.71
Washington	733	698	664	3.72	3.54	3.37	605	566	527	2.91	2.72	2.53
Oregon	69	85	100	.35	.43	.51	69	85	102	.33	.41	.49
California	3,454	3,145	2,836	17.53	15.96	14.40	3,885	3,531	3,176	18.68	16.98	15.27
Pacific	4,253	3,926	3,599	21.59	19.93	18.27	4,560	4,181	3,803	21.92	20.10	18.28
Hawaii	—	—	—	—	—	—	19	21	23	.09	.10	.11
Alaska	—	—	—	—	—	—	62	63	65	.30	.30	.31
United States	19,700	19,700	19,700	100.00	100.00	100.00	20,800	20,800	20,800	100.00	100.00	100.00

TABLE A-2—Continued

(Dollar amounts in millions)

State or Region	1957 Estimated Purchases β=.3	β=.2	β=.1	1957 v, in Percent β=.3	β=.2	β=.1	1958 Estimated Purchases β=.3	β=.2	β=.1	1958 v, in Percent β=.3	β=.2	β=.1
Maine	96	104	113	.40	.43	.47	122	128	134	.51	.53	.56
New Hampshire	53	59	65	.22	.25	.27	55	60	65	.23	.25	.27
Vermont	24	27	31	.10	.11	.13	31	35	38	.13	.15	.16
Massachusetts	854	850	847	3.56	3.55	3.53	958	935	912	4.01	3.91	3.82
Connecticut	1,232	1,157	1,082	5.13	4.82	4.51	992	918	844	4.15	3.84	3.53
Rhode Island	58	72	86	.24	.30	.36	53	67	81	.22	.28	.34
New England	2,317	2,271	2,226	9.66	9.47	9.28	2,211	2,143	2,074	9.22	8.92	8.64
New York	2,790	2,796	2,802	11.62	11.65	11.67	2,751	2,749	2,747	11.51	11.50	11.49
New Jersey	1,318	1,270	1,222	5.49	5.29	5.09	1,207	1,201	1,195	5.05	5.02	5.00
Pennsylvania	1,222	1,358	1,495	5.09	5.66	6.23	1,097	1,236	1,374	4.59	5.17	5.75
Middle Atlantic	5,329	5,423	5,517	22.20	22.60	22.99	5,055	5,187	5,318	21.15	21.70	22.25
Ohio	1,610	1,704	1,798	6.71	7.10	7.49	1,401	1,496	1,592	5.86	6.26	6.66
Indiana	734	734	734	3.06	3.06	3.06	607	631	655	2.54	2.64	2.74
Illinois	1,274	1,313	1,353	5.31	5.47	5.64	1,061	1,141	1,221	4.44	4.78	5.11
Michigan	775	937	1,099	3.23	3.91	4.58	856	994	1,133	3.58	4.16	4.74
Wisconsin	293	348	403	1.22	1.45	1.68	294	351	407	1.23	1.46	1.70
East North Central	4,687	5,038	5,388	19.53	20.99	22.45	4,219	4,613	5,008	17.66	19.31	20.96
Minnesota	228	246	264	.95	1.03	1.10	229	250	271	.96	1.05	1.14
Iowa	170	176	182	.71	.74	.76	146	165	184	.61	.69	.77
Missouri	540	534	528	2.25	2.23	2.20	588	576	564	2.46	2.41	2.36
North Dakota	26	26	26	.11	.11	.11	19	21	22	.08	.09	.09
South Dakota	10	12	14	.04	.05	.06	12	14	17	.05	.06	.07
Nebraska	53	56	60	.22	.23	.25	57	61	65	.24	.26	.27
Kansas	514	463	413	2.14	1.93	1.72	640	594	548	2.68	2.49	2.29
West North Central	1,541	1,516	1,490	6.43	6.32	6.21	1,690	1,680	1,670	7.07	7.03	6.99

Kentucky	101	120	139	.42	.50	.58	88	112	134	.37	.47	.56
Tennessee	161	191	221	.67	.80	.92	153	185	217	.64	.78	.91
Alabama	226	236	245	.94	.98	1.02	210	221	232	.88	.93	.97
Mississippi	94	97	101	.39	.40	.42	108	103	98	.45	.43	.41
East South Central	579	642	706	2.41	2.68	2.94	557	619	681	2.33	2.59	2.85
Arkansas	38	48	58	.16	.20	.24	36	46	55	.15	.19	.23
Oklahoma	173	167	161	.72	.69	.67	160	155	151	.67	.65	.63
Louisiana	197	205	214	.85	.85	.89	165	177	189	.69	.74	.79
Texas	1,233	1,198	1,163	5.14	4.99	4.85	1,224	1,188	1,152	5.12	4.97	4.82
West South Central	1,641	1,618	1,594	6.84	6.74	6.64	1,585	1,565	1,546	6.63	6.55	6.47
Delaware	67	79	91	.28	.33	.38	91	103	115	.38	.43	.48
Maryland	648	599	550	2.70	2.50	2.29	569	525	480	2.38	2.19	2.01
District of Columbia	72	73	74	.30	.31	.31	67	67	67	.28	.28	.28
Virginia	271	279	288	1.13	1.16	1.20	251	259	268	1.05	1.09	1.12
West Virginia	58	77	96	.24	.32	.40	74	91	108	.31	.38	.45
North Carolina	346	376	406	1.44	1.56	1.69	402	432	461	1.68	1.80	1.93
South Carolina	86	110	134	.36	.46	.56	86	110	134	.36	.46	.56
Georgia	324	327	331	1.34	1.36	1.38	325	333	342	1.36	1.40	1.43
Florida	230	235	240	.96	.98	1.00	337	324	311	1.41	1.36	1.30
South Atlantic	2,100	2,155	2,210	8.75	8.98	9.21	2,202	2,244	2,287	9.22	9.40	9.57
Montana	19	22	26	.08	.10	.11	24	27	31	.10	.11	.13
Idaho	14	18	22	.06	.07	.09	17	20	24	.07	.08	.10
Wyoming	19	19	19	.08	.08	.08	17	17	17	.07	.07	.07
Colorado	187	186	185	.78	.77	.77	191	186	182	.80	.78	.76
Utah	46	50	53	.19	.21	.22	65	66	67	.27	.28	.28
Nevada	12	12	12	.05	.05	.05	10	11	12	.04	.04	.05
Arizona	180	162	144	.75	.68	.60	208	187	165	.87	.78	.69
New Mexico	48	47	46	.20	.20	.19	60	58	57	.25	.24	.24
Mountain	523	514	506	2.18	2.14	2.11	590	572	555	2.47	2.39	2.32
Washington	718	656	593	2.99	2.73	2.47	894	809	724	3.74	3.39	3.03
Oregon	72	90	108	.30	.37	.45	72	92	112	.30	.39	.47
California	4,384	3,967	3,549	18.27	16.53	14.79	4,732	4,276	3,819	19.80	17.89	15.98
Pacific	5,173	4,711	4,248	21.56	19.63	17.70	5,696	5,175	4,654	23.84	21.66	19.48
Hawaii	29	31	34	.12	.13	.14	29	31	33	.12	.13	.14
Alaska	79	81	82	.33	.34	.34	74	75	76	.31	.31	.32
United States	24,000	24,000	24,000	100.00	100.00	100.00	23,900	23,900	23,900	100.00	100.00	100.00

TABLE A-2—Continued

(Dollar amounts in millions)

State or Region	1959 Estimated Purchases β=.3	β=.2	β=.1	1959 v, in Percent β=.3	β=.2	β=.1	1960 Estimated Purchases β=.3	β=.2	β=.1	1960 v, in Percent β=.3	β=.2	β=.1
Maine	92	99	105	.36	.39	.41	69	73	76	.28	.30	.33
New Hampshire	64	70	77	.25	.28	.30	80	84	88	.32	.34	.36
Vermont	26	28	30	.10	.11	.12	29	30	32	.12	.12	.13
Massachusetts	1,180	1,142	1,104	4.63	4.48	4.33	1,213	1,175	1,137	4.95	4.80	4.64
Connecticut	1,010	943	875	3.96	3.70	3.43	1,083	1,007	933	4.42	4.11	3.81
Rhode Island	54	69	84	.21	.27	.33	51	65	78	.21	.27	.32
New England	2,423	2,348	2,272	9.50	9.21	8.91	2,526	2,436	2,347	10.31	9.94	9.58
New York	2,815	2,820	2,825	11.04	11.06	11.08	2,804	2,803	2,801	11.44	11.44	11.43
New Jersey	1,380	1,371	1,362	5.41	5.38	5.34	1,308	1,296	1,284	5.34	5.29	5.24
Pennsylvania	1,132	1,273	1,415	4.44	4.99	5.54	1,118	1,252	1,387	4.57	5.11	5.66
Middle Atlantic	5,329	5,466	5,602	20.89	21.44	21.97	5,228	5,348	5,469	21.34	21.83	22.32
Ohio	1,461	1,571	1,680	5.73	6.16	6.59	1,323	1,440	1,558	5.40	5.88	6.36
Indiana	660	686	711	2.59	2.69	2.79	583	616	649	2.38	2.52	2.65
Illinois	1,051	1,150	1,250	4.12	4.51	4.90	985	1,073	1,161	4.02	4.38	4.74
Michigan	892	1,048	1,203	3.50	4.11	4.72	858	1,014	1,171	3.50	4.14	4.78
Wisconsin	319	381	444	1.25	1.49	1.74	316	370	424	1.29	1.51	1.73
East North Central	4,386	4,837	5,289	17.20	18.97	20.74	4,065	4,514	4,963	16.59	18.43	20.27
Minnesota	252	272	292	.99	1.07	1.15	245	263	282	1.00	1.07	1.15
Iowa	194	207	220	.76	.81	.86	191	201	210	.78	.82	.86
Missouri	629	621	613	2.47	2.44	2.41	505	500	495	2.06	2.04	2.02
North Dakota	3	4	5	.01	.02	.02	10	11	12	.04	.04	.05
South Dakota	26	27	28	.10	.10	.11	17	18	20	.07	.07	.08
Nebraska	74	75	77	.29	.29	.30	82	81	79	.33	.33	.32
Kansas	563	521	479	2.21	2.04	1.88	494	458	421	2.02	1.87	1.72
West North Central	1,741	1,728	1,715	6.83	6.78	6.73	1,544	1,531	1,517	6.30	6.25	6.19

Kentucky	94	119	143	.37	.47	.56	96	118	140	.39	.48	.57
Tennessee	166	199	232	.65	.78	.91	166	199	233	.68	.81	.95
Alabama	191	207	224	.75	.81	.88	159	178	196	.65	.72	.80
Mississippi	102	104	105	.40	.41	.41	93	96	98	.37	.39	.40
East South Central	553	630	703	2.17	2.47	2.76	512	588	666	2.09	2.40	2.72
Arkansas	38	49	59	.15	.19	.23	37	45	54	.15	.19	.22
Oklahoma	150	148	145	.59	.58	.57	134	133	132	.55	.54	.54
Louisiana	171	185	199	.67	.73	.78	159	170	181	.65	.70	.74
Texas	1,191	1,161	1,130	4.67	4.55	4.43	1,098	1,070	1,041	4.48	4.36	4.25
West South Central	1,550	1,540	1,530	6.08	6.04	6.00	1,426	1,417	1,408	5.82	5.78	5.74
Delaware	79	92	105	.31	.36	.41	61	73	86	.25	.30	.35
Maryland	627	585	543	2.46	2.30	2.13	546	515	483	2.23	2.10	1.97
District of Columbia	66	66	66	.26	.26	.26	71	70	69	.29	.28	.28
Virginia	337	345	354	1.32	1.35	1.39	407	412	417	1.66	1.68	1.70
West Virginia	74	95	117	.29	.37	.46	71	92	113	.29	.38	.46
North Carolina	339	371	403	1.33	1.45	1.58	298	328	358	1.22	1.34	1.46
South Carolina	89	114	140	.35	.45	.55	81	107	132	.33	.44	.54
Georgia	303	313	324	1.19	1.23	1.27	262	278	294	1.07	1.13	1.20
Florida	418	392	367	1.64	1.54	1.44	483	451	421	1.97	1.84	1.72
South Atlantic	2,333	2,376	2,420	9.15	9.32	9.49	2,283	2,326	2,371	9.32	9.50	9.68
Montana	28	30	33	.11	.12	.13	22	25	29	.09	.11	.12
Idaho	18	23	28	.07	.09	.11	29	33	37	.12	.13	.15
Wyoming	33	33	33	.13	.13	.13	20	21	22	.08	.09	.09
Colorado	232	222	212	.91	.87	.83	289	273	257	1.18	1.11	1.05
Utah	143	135	128	.56	.53	.50	175	166	157	.72	.68	.64
Nevada	10	11	13	.04	.04	.05	7	9	10	.03	.04	.04
Arizona	189	168	148	.74	.66	.58	223	203	184	.91	.83	.75
New Mexico	66	61	56	.26	.24	.22	69	64	59	.28	.26	.24
Mountain	717	682	648	2.81	2.67	2.54	834	796	757	3.41	3.25	3.09
Washington	974	891	808	3.82	3.50	3.17	789	715	642	3.22	2.92	2.62
Oregon	82	103	125	.32	.40	.49	74	94	113	.30	.38	.46
California	5,312	4,798	4,284	20.83	18.82	16.80	5,139	4,646	4,153	20.98	18.96	16.95
Pacific	6,367	5,792	5,217	24.97	22.71	20.46	6,000	5,454	4,910	24.49	22.26	20.04
Hawaii	31	33	36	.12	.13	.14	32	35	37	.13	.14	.15
Alaska	66	67	69	.26	.26	.27	54	55	56	.22	.23	.23
United States	25,500	25,500	25,500	100.00	100.00	100.00	24,500	24,500	24,500	100.00	100.00	100.00

TABLE A-2—Continued

(Dollar amounts in millions)

State or Region	1961 Estimated Purchases β=.3	β=.2	β=.1	1961 v, in Percent β=.3	β=.2	β=.1	1962 Estimated Purchases β=.3	β=.2	β=.1	1962 v, in Percent β=.3	β=.2	β=.1
Maine	92	99	105	.34	.37	.39	101	108	115	.34	.36	.39
New Hampshire	99	102	105	.37	.38	.39	98	101	104	.33	.34	.35
Vermont	33	34	35	.12	.13	.13	33	34	36	.11	.11	.12
Massachusetts	1,344	1,301	1,257	4.96	4.80	4.64	1,376	1,336	1,296	4.65	4.52	4.38
Connecticut	1,203	1,123	1,043	4.44	4.14	3.85	1,294	1,208	1,122	4.37	4.08	3.79
Rhode Island	62	75	89	.23	.28	.33	80	95	110	.27	.32	.37
New England	2,835	2,736	2,637	10.46	10.10	9.73	2,979	2,879	2,780	10.07	9.73	9.40
New York	3,032	3,030	3,029	11.19	11.18	11.18	3,072	3,091	3,111	10.38	10.45	10.51
New Jersey	1,432	1,394	1,357	5.27	5.14	5.01	1,566	1,533	1,501	5.29	5.18	5.07
Pennsylvania	1,295	1,435	1,575	4.78	5.29	5.81	1,444	1,584	1,723	4.88	5.35	5.82
Middle Atlantic	5,756	5,859	5,961	21.24	21.61	21.99	6,083	6,208	6,334	20.55	20.97	21.40
Ohio	1,352	1,476	1,600	4.99	5.44	5.90	1,545	1,681	1,817	5.22	5.68	6.14
Indiana	675	717	759	2.49	2.64	2.80	767	811	855	2.59	2.74	2.89
Illinois	1,076	1,181	1,285	3.97	4.36	4.74	1,151	1,270	1,388	3.89	4.29	4.69
Michigan	905	1,069	1,234	3.34	3.94	4.55	968	1,163	1,359	3.27	3.93	4.59
Wisconsin	360	423	485	1.33	1.56	1.79	400	468	536	1.35	1.58	1.81
East North Central	4,366	4,863	5,360	16.11	17.93	19.76	4,828	5,390	5,953	16.31	18.21	20.11
Minnesota	263	285	307	.97	1.05	1.13	311	334	358	1.05	1.13	1.21
Iowa	203	217	231	.75	.80	.85	216	227	237	.73	.77	.80
Missouri	560	562	564	2.07	2.07	2.08	633	635	636	2.14	2.15	2.15
North Dakota	35	35	35	.13	.13	.13	33	34	36	.11	.11	.12
South Dakota	46	48	49	.17	.18	.18	59	59	59	.20	.20	.20
Nebraska	89	87	86	.33	.32	.32	86	85	83	.29	.29	.28
Kansas	499	461	423	1.84	1.70	1.56	491	452	411	1.66	1.53	1.39
West North Central	1,694	1,693	1,692	6.25	6.24	6.24	1,829	1,826	1,823	6.18	6.17	6.16

Kentucky	103	129	154	.38	.48	.57	112	142	172	.38	.48	.58
Tennessee	201	238	274	.74	.88	1.02	237	278	320	.80	.94	1.08
Alabama	171	195	217	.63	.72	.80	216	234	252	.73	.79	.85
Mississippi	98	105	111	.36	.39	.41	115	121	127	.39	.41	.43
East South Central	572	666	759	2.11	2.46	2.80	678	773	869	2.29	2.61	2.94
Arkansas	73	81	89	.27	.30	.33	71	83	95	.24	.28	.32
Oklahoma	133	136	138	.49	.50	.51	148	146	145	.50	.49	.49
Louisiana	173	185	198	.64	.68	.73	225	233	240	.76	.79	.81
Texas	1,127	1,100	1,073	4.16	4.06	3.96	1,151	1,122	1,092	3.89	3.79	3.69
West South Central	1,504	1,502	1,499	5.55	5.54	5.53	1,595	1,585	1,575	5.39	5.36	5.32
Delaware	54	68	81	.20	.25	.30	62	75	89	.21	.25	.30
Maryland	602	566	531	2.22	2.09	1.96	616	588	559	2.08	1.99	1.89
District of Columbia	87	87	87	.32	.32	.32	124	124	124	.42	.42	.42
Virginia	477	480	482	1.76	1.77	1.78	482	485	488	1.63	1.64	1.65
West Virginia	81	104	127	.30	.38	.47	127	151	175	.43	.51	.59
North Carolina	341	378	415	1.26	1.39	1.53	352	400	447	1.19	1.35	1.51
South Carolina	95	123	152	.35	.46	.56	118	150	182	.40	.51	.61
Georgia	301	320	339	1.11	1.18	1.25	397	417	437	1.34	1.41	1.47
Florida	602	560	518	2.22	2.06	1.91	625	577	530	2.11	1.95	1.79
South Atlantic	2,640	2,686	2,733	9.74	9.91	10.09	2,906	2,970	3,034	9.82	10.04	10.25
Montana	49	53	57	.18	.19	.21	50	53	56	.17	.18	.19
Idaho	24	30	35	.09	.11	.13	27	33	38	.09	.11	.13
Wyoming	19	20	22	.07	.07	.08	50	51	53	.17	.17	.18
Colorado	401	378	355	1.48	1.39	1.31	426	406	385	1.44	1.37	1.30
Utah	239	226	214	.88	.83	.79	326	305	284	1.10	1.03	.96
Nevada	14	14	14	.05	.05	.05	9	10	12	.03	.03	.04
Arizona	211	190	168	.78	.70	.62	228	204	181	.77	.69	.61
New Mexico	62	58	54	.23	.21	.20	68	62	56	.23	.21	.19
Mountain	1,019	969	919	3.76	3.57	3.39	1,181	1,122	1,063	3.99	3.79	3.59
Washington	846	756	667	3.12	2.79	2.46	1,057	948	841	3.57	3.20	2.84
Oregon	84	105	127	.31	.39	.47	89	112	136	.30	.38	.46
California	5,705	5,183	4,661	21.05	19.13	17.20	6,296	5,704	5,112	21.27	19.27	17.27
Pacific	6,637	6,046	5,455	24.49	22.32	20.15	7,439	6,764	6,089	25.13	22.85	20.57
Hawaii	30	34	38	.11	.13	.14	33	36	38	.11	.12	.13
Alaska	54	55	57	.20	.21	.21	50	50	50	.17	.17	.17
United States	27,100	27,100	27,100	100.00	100.00	100.00	29,600	29,600	29,600	100.00	100.00	100.00

Source: Calculated from sources of procurement data listed for Table 5 on the basis of three alternative assumptions about the geographic dispersion of procurement expenditures (see Chap. V).

TABLE A–3. Military Wages and Salaries, by State and Region, 1947–62

(Millions of dollars)

State or Region	1947	1948	1949	1950	1951	1952	1953
Maine	8	10	12	8	22	33	43
New Hampshire	9	9	11	7	12	16	16
Vermont	2	2	2	2	5	7	7
Massachusetts	66	73	85	104	182	212	205
Connecticut	20	23	24	24	40	44	45
Rhode Island	39	37	42	51	77	99	102
New England	144	154	175	195	338	410	418
New York	152	143	124	131	257	334	332
New Jersey	130	136	123	116	194	246	246
Pennsylvania	94	83	72	81	162	212	194
Middle Atlantic	376	362	319	328	613	792	772
Ohio	61	59	50	48	105	145	148
Indiana	23	21	19	30	102	98	102
Illinois	116	136	130	154	238	273	240
Michigan	47	40	38	49	94	121	106
Wisconsin	15	14	13	19	68	66	40
East North Central	262	269	252	301	609	702	637
Minnesota	13	14	13	13	31	38	38
Iowa	13	10	9	8	20	26	27
Missouri	26	24	18	34	115	127	131
North Dakota	2	2	2	2	6	7	7
South Dakota	6	7	9	12	19	27	28
Nebraska	12	13	13	15	24	31	32
Kansas	32	48	66	58	83	116	147
West North Central	104	118	129	142	297	372	410
Kentucky	56	98	89	120	216	233	218
Tennessee	32	39	37	42	75	94	91
Alabama	40	34	30	45	125	143	148
Mississippi	32	26	32	53	82	87	89
East South Central	160	197	188	260	498	557	546

166

TABLE A–3—*Continued*

(Millions of dollars)

State or Region	1947	1948	1949	1950	1951	1952	1953
Arkansas	17	24	28	18	56	65	67
Oklahoma	32	37	42	55	96	126	120
Louisiana	35	35	35	59	117	154	156
Texas	193	201	307	410	601	737	742
West South Central	277	297	412	542	870	1,082	1,085
Delaware	2	2	2	4	11	13	15
Mary'and	94	95	105	140	230	312	304
District of Columbia	53	55	56	65	71	79	74
Virginia	269	264	292	346	554	668	662
West Virginia	11	10	7	6	15	18	17
North Carolina	104	114	134	177	262	280	275
South Carolina	66	91	78	81	208	215	189
Georgia	71	79	111	136	239	282	265
Florida	136	100	114	136	214	306	333
South Atlantic	806	810	899	1,091	1,804	2,173	2,134
Montana	5	6	10	9	15	19	20
Idaho	2	3	5	2	11	23	18
Wyoming	7	10	19	21	25	32	30
Colorado	41	33	43	65	106	116	108
Utah	7	7	6	11	18	18	18
Nevada	1	2	5	9	12	19	25
Arizona	18	19	23	26	47	70	67
New Mexico	20	21	30	41	59	87	96
Mountain	101	101	141	184	293	384	382
Washington	113	109	152	175	212	236	249
Oregon	12	10	10	12	26	31	29
California	464	453	463	596	1,016	1,325	1,274
Pacific	589	572	625	783	1,254	1,592	1,552
Hawaii	80	79	72	71	99	125	129
Alaska	—	—	—	84	112	137	148
United States	2,901	2,961	3,212	3,981	6,785	8,326	8,212

TABLE A–3—Continued

(Millions of dollars)

State or Region	1954	1955	1956	1957	1958	1959	1960	1961	1962
Maine	54	53	56	59	64	65	72	73	73
New Hampshire	17	16	23	27	33	40	39	40	42
Vermont	8	6	7	8	9	8	6	4	5
Massachusetts	191	182	184	200	204	206	207	209	210
Connecticut	44	45	48	50	54	61	65	66	63
Rhode Island	104	105	105	93	103	103	88	92	102
New England	418	407	424	437	466	484	477	485	495
New York	346	337	318	281	282	308	304	289	311
New Jersey	248	208	182	188	215	224	230	237	244
Pennsylvania	162	167	164	150	149	152	154	152	158
Middle Atlantic	756	712	664	619	646	684	688	678	713
Ohio	142	137	145	138	148	155	152	152	161
Indiana	61	50	57	55	55	62	66	66	72
Illinois	258	266	268	238	240	249	255	269	275
Michigan	99	97	101	99	103	109	117	134	147
Wisconsin	41	38	43	44	46	48	47	46	48
East North Central	601	588	613	574	592	622	636	667	703
Minnesota	41	39	42	39	39	42	43	43	47
Iowa	28	26	27	25	26	26	24	24	26
Missouri	143	137	129	122	133	142	140	143	148
North Dakota	7	7	7	8	8	15	24	33	41
South Dakota	30	26	26	25	29	31	26	23	26
Nebraska	39	48	53	53	60	68	72	76	85
Kansas	145	144	147	146	153	156	157	163	168
West North Central	433	427	431	419	449	479	486	504	542
Kentucky	194	202	149	150	168	174	188	197	215
Tennessee	84	84	92	88	97	96	94	94	101
Alabama	114	114	116	114	120	118	120	119	125
Mississippi	94	88	83	71	77	93	102	111	125
East South Centra	486	488	440	423	462	481	504	521	566

168

TABLE A–3—*Continued*

(Millions of dollars)

State or Region	1954	1955	1956	1957	1958	1959	1960	1961	1962
Arkansas	70	68	78	86	71	57	47	56	81
Oklahoma	120	119	123	127	139	141	138	136	151
Louisiana	125	100	138	149	138	121	106	114	163
Texas	768	739	705	683	681	695	725	721	773
West South Central	1,083	1,026	1,044	1,045	1,029	1,014	1,016	1,027	1,168
Delaware	22	26	29	32	32	31	34	33	35
Maryland	297	291	292	272	257	271	250	252	267
District of Columbia	73	75	80	72	78	83	77	77	82
Virginia	604	557	548	551	518	548	504	508	539
West Virginia	18	17	17	17	15	16	15	15	15
North Carolina	282	284	269	275	274	291	297	310	351
South Carolina	197	182	186	196	191	214	214	218	223
Georgia	298	289	269	283	279	290	297	295	343
Florida	320	318	347	360	367	362	345	356	367
South Atlantic	2,111	2,039	2,037	2,058	2,011	2,106	2,033	2,064	2,222
Montana	20	19	22	22	24	27	31	35	39
Idaho	19	16	18	19	21	23	24	25	28
Wyoming	31	30	37	25	14	9	12	15	17
Colorado	141	139	148	139	128	121	121	123	163
Utah	22	23	19	17	18	19	21	22	24
Nevada	30	29	28	31	30	30	32	34	35
Arizona	75	88	85	88	89	88	80	79	86
New Mexico	95	90	87	90	98	97	96	88	95
Mountain	433	434	444	431	422	414	417	421	487
Washington	246	239	236	233	224	226	236	247	273
Oregon	29	27	27	26	28	34	34	33	34
California	1,113	1,109	1,130	1,112	1,152	1,193	1,220	1,241	1,309
Pacific	1,388	1,375	1,393	1,371	1,404	1,453	1,490	1,521	1,616
Hawaii	129	145	165	173	169	174	175	180	192
Alaska	147	149	143	143	120	113	138	120	121
United States	7,983	7,789	7,800	7,694	7,771	8,024	8,058	8,187	8,823

Source: U. S. Office of Business Economics, *Personal Income by States since 1929*, a supplement to the *Survey of Current Business* (1956), and articles on personal income by state (variously titled) in *Survey of Current Business*, Vols. 39–43 (August issues, 1959–63). See also the appendix to Chap. V.

TABLE A–4. Department of Defense Civilian Wages and Salaries, by State and Region, 1947–62

(Millions of dollars)

State or Region	1947	1948	1949	1950	1951	1952	1953
Maine	9	10	9	8	20	23	20
New Hamsphire	9	10	10	8	20	24	21
Vermont	a	a	a	a	a	1	1
Massachusetts	51	57	64	65	112	157	152
Connecticut	4	4	5	5	8	8	13
Rhode Island	20	22	22	22	32	35	37
New England	93	103	110	108	192	248	244
New York	145	145	150	148	258	342	322
New Jersey	57	58	66	71	108	141	160
Pennsylvania	159	168	179	182	298	344	341
Middle Atlantic	361	371	395	401	664	827	823
Ohio	91	90	114	123	210	226	225
Indiana	22	26	28	25	43	81	80
Illinois	60	65	73	80	130	175	151
Michigan	15	16	23	27	45	65	52
Wisconsin	3	3	3	3	6	9	9
East North Central	191	200	241	258	434	556	517
Minnesota	4	5	5	5	5	6	7
Iowa	2	2	2	2	2	4	18
Missouri	45	43	42	44	67	42	53
North Dakota	1	2	3	3	4	4	3
South Dakota	3	3	3	4	7	7	8
Nebraska	12	17	17	15	25	26	30
Kansas	13	11	10	12	19	27	30
West North Central	80	83	82	85	129	116	149
Kentucky	21	24	24	26	42	57	56
Tennessee	22	25	23	26	35	39	40
Alabama	38	39	37	42	74	113	123
Mississippi	17	16	17	17	23	24	24
East South Central	98	104	101	111	174	233	243

170

TABLE A–4—Continued

(Millions of dollars)

State or Region	1947	1948	1949	1950	1951	1952	1953
Arkansas	8	10	10	10	18	19	27
Oklahoma	43	50	51	59	92	111	115
Louisiana	24	25	27	17	21	36	38
Texas	111	119	121	119	206	258	253
West South Central	186	204	209	205	337	424	433
Delaware	ᵃ	ᵃ	ᵃ	1	2	2	3
Maryland	92	106	112	120	164	199	210
District of Columbia	99	114	120	127	188	195	169
Virginia	163	187	198	215	321	337	348
West Virginia	4	6	6	6	9	8	6
North Carolina	25	25	22	22	15	37	39
South Carolina	31	33	30	29	51	57	58
Georgia	50	53	54	60	103	127	126
Florida	58	55	55	55	78	94	99
South Atlantic	522	579	597	635	931	1,056	1,058
Montana	2	2	3	2	3	3	2
Idaho	3	3	2	1	3	5	6
Wyoming	2	2	3	3	5	5	7
Colorado	16	17	18	20	44	65	66
Utah	32	45	44	46	77	98	100
Nevada	4	4	4	7	10	11	12
Arizona	8	8	8	10	15	20	20
New Mexico	8	8	11	14	21	22	31
Mountain	75	89	93	103	178	229	244
Washington	80	78	94	107	172	202	171
Oregon	10	15	12	13	20	25	19
California	362	364	401	414	654	740	724
Pacific	452	457	507	534	846	967	914
Hawaii	—	—	—	—	—	—	—
Alaska	—	—	—	—	—	—	—
United States	2,060	2,187	2,333	2,439	3,883	4,657	4,622

171

TABLE A–4—Continued

(Millions of dollars)

State or Region	1954	1955	1956	1957	1958	1959	1960	1961	1962
Maine	20	22	21	23	26	31	36	35	36
New Hampshire	23	19	20	22	25	30	36	36	36
Vermont	1	1	1	1	1	1	1	1	1
Massachusetts	130	140	140	145	151	186	161	180	182
Connecticut	9	12	12	13	14	15	17	17	18
Rhode Island	40	40	41	42	43	45	46	50	50
New England	223	234	235	246	260	308	297	319	324
New York	268	300	311	306	316	316	316	328	327
New Jersey	127	139	151	158	167	169	176	187	200
Pennsylvania	327	334	335	339	363	370	383	403	449
Middle Atlantic	722	773	797	803	846	855	875	918	976
Ohio	196	222	233	240	238	236	232	256	259
Indiana	77	69	67	64	63	61	62	67	75
Illinois	151	143	141	142	150	152	153	160	173
Michigan	40	49	51	52	57	60	62	66	91
Wisconsin	7	8	10	10	10	11	12	11	14
East North Central	471	491	502	508	518	520	521	560	612
Minnesota	7	8	8	11	10	10	12	11	13
Iowa	2	17	17	18	22	19	19	21	24
Missouri	59	58	63	53	71	73	73	78	85
North Dakota	3	3	3	3	3	4	4	4	7
South Dakota	6	10	8	8	8	8	9	11	12
Nebraska	31	27	25	23	24	24	26	28	27
Kansas	33	33	37	39	38	35	34	35	34
West North Central	141	156	161	155	176	173	177	188	202
Kentucky	39	50	53	54	57	55	51	65	68
Tennessee	41	47	47	47	48	50	46	46	48
Alabama	129	132	157	187	203	219	219	215	220
Mississippi	24	29	31	39	34	35	39	35	38
East South Central	233	258	288	327	342	359	355	361	374

TABLE A–4—Continued

(Millions of dollars)

State or Region	1954	1955	1956	1957	1958	1959	1960	1961	1962
Arkansas	22	24	25	25	25	23	22	31	30
Oklahoma	116	112	120	118	130	132	134	138	149
Louisiana	32	33	39	40	40	35	34	35	44
Texas	256	257	301	309	308	312	316	331	359
West South Central	426	426	485	492	503	502	506	535	582
Delaware	3	5	7	7	7	7	4	8	8
Maryland	209	236	243	262	300	313	325	349	367
District of Columbia	169	194	194	172	175	175	174	144	168
Virginia	329	356	369	392	412	424	441	473	531
West Virginia	6	5	6	6	7	7	7	8	6
North Carolina	41	39	43	45	47	41	52	55	59
South Carolina	59	57	63	66	70	75	82	84	92
Georgia	144	132	140	135	154	164	165	170	184
Florida	129	108	127	136	137	141	141	147	155
South Atlantic	1,089	1,132	1,192	1,221	1,309	1,347	1,391	1,438	1,570
Montana	3	3	4	3	4	4	5	7	8
Idaho	4	4	4	4	5	4	3	4	3
Wyoming	6	6	7	7	6	4	4	3	4
Colorado	70	66	69	70	73	75	77	81	89
Utah	84	85	87	85	94	97	99	107	119
Nevada	12	12	15	16	15	16	16	16	16
Arizona	24	27	33	30	38	40	42	38	48
New Mexico	35	35	42	47	53	55	58	60	61
Mountain	238	238	261	262	288	295	304	316	348
Washington	156	163	163	155	155	151	146	177	157
Oregon	15	19	20	20	20	22	22	23	23
California	650	721	751	764	804	837	862	922	975
Pacific	821	902	934	939	979	1,010	1,030	1,122	1,155
Hawaii	—	—	—	—	—	106	115	119	123
Alaska	—	—	—	—	—	45	46	48	49
United States	4,362	4,613	4,857	4,952	5,218	5,520	5,618	5,922	6,315

Source: U. S. Office of Business Economics. The data are unpublished detail of the state personal income statistics, save 1947, 1948, and 1954, which I estimated on the basis of employment distributions also obtained from that office. The figures have been adjusted, in some cases by the OBE and in a few cases by myself, so that they reflect the residence of employees where that differs from the physical location of employment; these adjustments are on the basis of census information on residence and occupation, on commuter patterns, and in some cases on interpolations. See also the appendix to Chap. V.

[a] Less than $.5 million.

Bibliography

Aerospace Industries Association of America, *Aerospace Year Book.* Washington: The Association, 1961.

Bolton, Roger E., ed., *Defense and Disarmament: The Economics of Transition.* Englewood Cliffs, New Jersey: Prentice-Hall, Inc., 1966.

Committee for Economic Development, Southern California Associates, *National Defense and Southern California, 1961-1970* (including a Research Report by George A. Steiner). Los Angeles: Committee for Economic Development, Southern California Associates, 1961. 136 pp.

Cunningham, William Glenn, *The Aircraft Industry: A Study in Industrial Location.* Los Angeles: L. L. Morrison, 1951. 247 pp.

"Defense Expenditures Abroad," *Survey of Current Business,* Vol. 39, November 1959. pp. 15-17.

"Defense Industry Lacks Plans for Civilian Production," *The New York Times,* August 16, 1963. p. 31.

Duesenberry, James S., *Income, Saving and the Theory of Consumer Behavior.* Harvard Economic Series, Vol. 87. Cambridge: Harvard University Press, 1949. 128 pp.

Duncombe, Bruce F., *Upper Midwest Commodity Flows, 1958,* Technical Paper No. 3. Minneapolis: Upper Midwest Economic Study, 1962. 51 pp.

"Foreign Countries Earn $2.5 Billion from United States Military Outlays in 1953," *Survey of Current Business,* Vol. 34, August 1954. pp. 7-8.

"GNP by Major Industries, 1958-1962 Revised and Updated," *Survey of Current Business,* Vol. 43, September 1963. pp. 9-10.

Haavelmo, Trygve, "Methods of Measuring the Marginal Propensity to Consume," *Journal of the American Statistical Association,* Vol. 42,

March 1947. pp. 105-22. (Reprinted in William Hood and Tjalling Koopmans, eds. *Studies in Econometric Method.* New York: Wiley, 1953. 323 pp.)

Hansen, W. Lee and Tiebout, Charles M., "An Intersectoral Flows Analysis of the California Economy," *Review of Economics and Statistics,* Vol. 45, November 1963. pp. 409-18.

Hildebrand, George H. and Mace, Arthur, Jr., "The Employment Multiplier in An Expanding Industrial Market: Los Angeles County, 1940-1947," *Review of Economics and Statistics,* Vol. 32, August 1950. pp. 241-49.

Hirsch, Werner Z., ed., *Elements of Regional Accounts.* Baltimore: Johns Hopkins, 1964. 221 pp.

Isard, Walter, *Methods of Regional Analysis.* Cambridge: Technology Press of the Massachusetts Institute of Technology, 1960. 784 pp.

Isard, Walter and Ganschow, James, *Awards of Prime Military Contracts by County, State and Metropolitan Area of the United States, Fiscal Year 1960.* Philadelphia: Regional Science Research Institute, undated.

Kendall, Maurice G. and Stuart, Alan, *The Advanced Theory of Statistics,* Vol. 1. London: C. Griffin, 1958.

Marimont, Martin L., "GNP by Major Industries," *Survey of Current Business,* Vol. 42, October 1962. pp. 6-18.

Metzler, Lloyd A., "A Multiple-Region Theory of Income and Trade," *Econometrica,* Vol. 18, October 1950. pp. 329-354.

Mushkin, Selma J., "Distribution of Federal Expenditures Among the States," *Review of Economics and Statistics,* Vol. 39, November 1957. pp. 435-450.

National Bureau of Economic Research, *Regional Income. Studies in Income and Wealth,* Vol. 21. Princeton: Princeton University Press, 1957. 408 pp.

"National Income and Product Accounts," *Survey of Current Business,* Vols. 42-43, July issues 1962-63.

Peck, Merton J. and Scherer, Frederic M., *The Weapons Acquisition Process: An Economic Analysis.* Boston: Graduate School of Business Administration, Harvard University, 1962. 736 pp.

Personal Income by State, Articles on (variously titled), *Survey of Current Business,* Vols. 39-43, August issues 1959-63.

Pfister, Richard L., *Military Expenditures in New England,* Federal Reserve Bank of Boston, Research Report No. 14. Boston: The Bank, 1961.

Shepler, Cora E., "United States Defense Expenditures Abroad," *Survey of Current Business,* Vol. 42, January 1962. pp. 14-16.

"Space Age Boom Is Bringing a Revolution to the Southwest," *The New York Times,* August 25, 1963. p. 56.

Theil, Henri, *Economic Forecasts and Policy,* 2nd ed., rev. Amsterdam: North-Holland, 1961.

U. S. Bureau of the Census, *U. S. Annual Survey of Manufactures: 1959 and 1960.* Washington: Government Printing Office, 1963. 464 pp.

————, *U. S. Annual Survey of Manufactures: 1961.* Washington: Government Printing Office, 1963. 480 pp.

————, *U. S. Census of Manufactures: 1958.* Vols. 1-3. Washington: Government Printing Office, 1963. 464 pp.

U. S. Bureau of Employment Security, *Employment and Wages of Workers Covered by State Unemployment Insurance Laws,* special issue of *Statistical Supplement to Labor Market and Employment Security,* annual issues 1947-49 and quarterly issues 1950-62. Washington: Office of Program Review and Analysis. Processed.

————, *Missiles and Aircraft, Labor Market Developments.* Industry Manpower Survey No. 102. Washington: Office of Program Review and Analysis, 1962. Processed. 20 pp.

U. S. Congress. House of Representatives. Appropriations Committee. *Air Force Intercontinental Ballistic Missile Base Construction Program.* Hearings 87 Cong. 1 sess. Washington: Government Printing Office, 1961. 310 pp.

————, *Department of Defense Appropriations for 1959, Procurement, Supply, and Surplus Operations.* Hearings 85 Cong. 2 sess. Washington: Government Printing Office, 1958. 479 pp.

————. *Department of Defense Appropriations for 1960, Part 5.* Hearings 86 Cong. 1 sess. Washington: Government Printing Office, 1959. 864 pp.

————. *Department of Defense Appropriations for 1961, Part 5.* Hearings 86 Cong. 2 sess. Washington: Government Printing Office, 1960. 942 pp.

————. *Department of Defense Appropriations for 1962, Part 5.* Hearings 87 Cong. 1 sess. Washington: Government Printing Office, 1961. 717 pp.

————. *Department of Defense Appropriations for 1963, Part 4.* Hearings 87 Cong. 2 sess. Washington: Government Printing Office, 1962. 665 pp.

U. S. Congress. House of Representatives. Armed Services Committee. *Utilization of Naval Shipyard Facilities.* Hearings 87 Cong. 1 sess. Washington: Government Printing Office, 1961. 200 pp.

U. S. Congress. House of Representatives. Select Committee on Small

Business. *The Aircraft Industry*. Hearings 84 Cong. 2 sess. Washington: Government Printing Office, 1956. 306 pp.

———. *The Aircraft Industry*. Hearings 85 Cong. 2 sess. Washington: Government Printing Office, 1959. 212 pp.

U. S. Congress. Joint Economic Committee. *Background Material on Economic Aspects of Military Procurement and Supply*. 86 Cong. 2 sess. Washington: Government Printing Office, 1960. 236 pp.

———. *Impact of Defense Procurement*. Hearings 86 Cong. 2 sess. Washington: Government Printing Office, 1960. 594 pp.

———. *Inventory Fluctuations and Economic Stabilization*. Hearings 87 Cong. 2 sess. Washington: Government Printing Office, 1962. 263 pp.

———. *January 1961 Economic Report of the President and Economic Situation and Outlook*. Hearings 87 Cong. 1 sess. Washington: Government Printing Office, 1961. 725 pp.

U. S. Congress. Senate. Appropriations Committee. *Department of Defense Appropriations for 1959*. Hearings 85 Cong. 2 sess. Washington: Government Printing Office, 1958. 1368 pp.

———. *Department of Defense Appropriations for 1960*. Hearings 86 Cong. 1 sess. Washington: Government Printing Office, 1959. 1660 pp.

———. *Department of Defense Appropriations for 1961*. Hearings 86 Cong. 2 sess. Washington: Government Printing Office, 1960. 1853 pp.

———. *Department of Defense Appropriations for 1962*. Hearings 87 Cong. 1 sess. Washington: Government Printing Office, 1961. 1709 pp.

———. *Department of Defense Appropriations for 1963*. Hearings 87 Cong. 2 sess. Washington: Government Printing Office, 1962. 1849 pp.

U. S. Congress. Senate. Armed Services Committee. *Military Construction Authorization, Fiscal Year 1959*. Hearings 85 Cong. 2 sess. Washington: Government Printing Office, 1958. 1096 pp.

———. *Military Procurement*. Hearings 86 Cong. 1 sess. Washington: Government Printing Office, 1959. 671 pp.

U. S. Congress. Senate. Select Committee on Small Business. *Impact of Defense Spending on Labor Surplus Areas, 1962*. Hearings 87 Cong. 2 sess. Washington: Government Printing Office, 1962. 204 pp.

———. *Military Procurement*. Hearings 83 Cong. 1 sess. Washington: Government Printing Office, 1953. 535 pp.

———. *Small Business Participation in Defense Subcontracting*. Hearings 86 Cong. 1 sess. Washington: Government Printing Office, 1959. 317 pp.

U. S. Department of Defense, *Annual Report on Purchases under the Armed Services Procurement Act of 1947, Fiscal Year 1950.* Washington: Munitions Board. Processed.

————, *Annual Report on Purchases under the Armed Services Procurement Act of 1947, Fiscal Year 1951.* Washington: Munitions Board. Processed.

————, *The Changing Patterns of Defense Procurement.* Washington: Office of the Secretary of Defense, 1962. Processed. 21 pp.

————, *Five-Year Trends in Defense Procurement, 1958-1962.* Washington: Office of the Secretary of Defense, 1963. Processed. 62 pp.

————, *Military Prime Contract Awards in Areas of Substantial Unemployment,* quarterly issues, 1957-64. Washington: Office of the Secretary of Defense. Processed.

————, *Military Prime Contract Awards by Region and State, Fiscal Years 1962, 1963, and 1964.* Washington: Office of the Secretary of Defense, 1965. Processed. 71 pp.

————, *Military Prime Contract Awards by State,* quarterly issues, 1951-62. Washington: Office of the Secretary of Defense. Processed.

————, *Military Prime Contract Awards and Subcontract Payments,* quarterly issues, 1955-64. Washington: Office of the Secretary of Defense. Processed.

————, *Net Value of Military Prime Contract Construction Awards, by State, Fiscal Years 1952-1961.* Washington: Office of the Secretary of Defense, 1962. Processed. 1 p.

————, *Status of Funds by Budget Category, Military Functions, Fiscal Years 1951-1954.* Washington: Office of the Secretary of Defense, 1955. Processed.

U. S. Library of Congress, *Federal Taxation and Expenditures in the Several States,* by I. M. Labovitz. Washington: Legislative Reference Service, 1959. Processed.

U. S. National Aeronautics and Space Administration, *Annual Procurement Report, Fiscal Year 1961.* Washington: The Administration. Processed.

U. S. Office of Business Economics, *Personal Income by States since 1929,* a supplement to the *Survey of Current Business.* Washington: Government Printing Office, 1956. 229 pp.

————, *United States Income and Output,* a supplement to the *Survey of Current Business.* Washington: Government Printing Office, 1958. 241 pp.

U. S. Public Health Service, *Statistical Materials on the Distribution of Federal Expenditures Among the States,* by Selma J. Mushkin. Washington: Division of Public Health Methods, 1956. Processed. 79 pp.

Upper Midwest Economic Study, *The Geographical Impact of the Federal Budget,* Technical Paper No. 3. Minneapolis: The Study, 1962. Processed. 27 pp.

Weidenbaum, Murray L., *Government Spending: Process and Measurement.* n. p., 1958. Processed. Various paging.

Index

Index*